Evelyn Waugn

Brief Lives:
Evelyn Waugh

Michael Barber

For Leo Cooper, who recruited me

Brief Lives
Published by Hesperus Press Limited
28 Mortimer Street, London W1W 7RD
www.hesperuspress.com

First published by Hesperus Press Limited, 2013

Designed and typeset by Fraser Muggeridge studio
Printed and bound in Great Britain by CPI Group (UK) Ltd

ISBN: 978-1-84391-927-8

Contents

Author's note

Evelyn Waugh hated the promiscuous use of Christian names, so he would have bridled at my calling him 'Evelyn' here. To begin with I thought of following Martin Stannard's lead and calling him 'Evelyn' as a boy and 'Waugh' as a grown-up, but then decided that in a short book such a solution would merely confuse the reader. This is why, like other members of the Waugh family, he is known by his Christian name.

Preface

Lunching one day at the Beefsteak club with the historian Hugh Trevor-Roper, Christopher Sykes spoke of the 'terrible difficulty' of writing the life of a man 'whose every action showed him to be a *shit*'. The man in question was his old friend, Evelyn Waugh, probably the most paradoxical figure in modern English liter ature. Waugh wrote some of the funniest passages in the English language, yet for the last twenty years of his life he suffered from chronic melancholia. Again, he gave away large sums of money to Catholic charities and, unprompted, went out of his way to commend other writers whose work he admired; yet he was also a merciless bully, particularly of those who were not equipped to answer back. In later life he behaved like a country gentleman, but spoilt the effect by dressing like a bookie in loud check suits and a grey bowler hat. His second home was White's club in St James's, yet his intimates were tough, opinionated females like Nancy Mitford, Ann Fleming and Diana Cooper. And so disillusioned did he become with his one-time favourite novel, *Brideshead Revisited*, that he mocked it in the final volume of his war trilogy, *Sword of Honour.*

Sykes's 'terrible difficulty' was all too apparent to Kingsley Amis, who began his review of the biography by saying that this book reinforced his thankfulness that he never met Evelyn Waugh. But would Waugh have written so well had he not been such a shit? Amis – of whom one could ask the same question – thought not: '[W]ithout this compulsion to say the unsayable he would never have come to be the writer he was.' John Carey, writing later, made a similar point: 'The acid refinement of his style required a certain part of his brain to remain dead. His blanket denunciation of fellow humans would have been impossible for a fully formed intelligence.' He was at his best with rogues like Basil Seal and Captain Grimes. When he tried to create a righteous character like the saintly Mr Crouchback senior, he asked too much of his readers: the old man was simply too good to be true.

Waugh's friends, all of whom knew how badly he could behave, forgave him his trespasses because they were outweighed by his qualities. 'What a monster!' wrote Nancy Mitford. 'How I miss him!' She died before the publication of his diaries reawakened an interest in his life and work that continues to this day. Whether this would have flattered Waugh himself is another matter. When an inoffensive American woman with whom he was dining praised *Brideshead Revisited*, he replied: 'I thought it was good myself, but now that I know that a common, boring American woman like yourself admires it, I am not so sure.' No wonder Waugh's fellow novelist, Anthony Powell, told Sykes, 'It's impossible to be objective about Evelyn.'

Childhood and Schooldays
1903–21

'A weird mixture of faith and frivolity'
Arthur Waugh's description of Evelyn as a boy.

Arthur Evelyn St John Waugh was born in Hampstead on 28 October 1903, the second son of Arthur Waugh, a publisher and man of letters, and Catherine, née Raban, his wife. His parents had hoped for a daughter, hence his mother's whimsical decision to call him Evelyn, an epicene name he never liked and one that probably contributed to his subsequent pugnacity. But the arrival of another boy in the family delighted his brother Alec, already at five a keen cricketer. 'Splendid,' he said to his father. 'Now we'll have a wicket-keeper.'

He was wrong.

Evelyn grew up to detest organized games, particularly cricket. That his brother should have devoted so many hours to playing and watching them was to Evelyn incomprehensible. Indeed all he and Alec had in common, besides their parents, was an aptitude for storytelling. Late in life Evelyn made the somewhat specious claim that although 'antithetical', they were not 'antipathetical'. What is certain is that it was thanks to Alec that in 1928 he became a client of the legendary literary agent A.D. Peters, his prop and stay for almost forty years.

Evelyn described himself as 'a quarter Scotch', but if you go back far enough you find that most of his forbears began their journey to the West Country, where his father and mother grew up, from north of the border. They belonged to the professional classes – lawyers, doctors, clergymen, soldiers and civil servants. Among them was Lord Cockburn, Evelyn's great-great-grandfather, the distinguished judge whose portrait used to be on Scottish banknotes. His title did not impress his descendant, who said he would like to have been descended from 'a useless Lord', not one ennobled for 'practical reasons'.

Mention must also be made of Evelyn's paternal grandfather, Dr Alexander Waugh (1840–1906), known to his descendants as 'the Brute'. In the vicinity of Midsomer Norton, near Bath, where he practised, Dr Waugh was a popular figure, bluff, gregarious, active in local affairs and a first-class shot. But his family lived in terror of this squat, bewhiskered tyrant whose bite was worse than his bark. On one infamous occasion he and his wife Anne were in their carriage when a wasp settled on her forehead. Using the knob of the whip he always carried he squashed the wasp, thus ensuring that it stung Anne. Did Evelyn inherit his sadistic streak from the Brute? It seems reasonable to suppose so.

The Brute had five legitimate children, two sons and three daughters. The girls never married, living together in the family home where Evelyn, as a boy, would visit them. Alick, the younger son, a bit of a rebel, took the drastic step of going to sea at the age of twelve to escape his father's floggings. He died young of malaria. That left Arthur (1866–1943), an asthmatic whose infirmity stayed the Brute's hand, but not his determination to make a man of his 'pale and peaky' heir. Arthur was left stranded up trees, ordered out of bed and sent on errands in the dark and swung violently back and forth on farm gates. The upshot was that although he did not lack for grit, he suffered dreadfully from 'nerves' all his life.

And yet Arthur not only admired his father, he also shared two of his passions: cricket and amateur dramatics. Thanks to his asthma he was never much good at cricket, which was why he took such vicarious pleasure in his elder son, Alec's, achievements. His asthma also ruled out any hopes of a career on the stage, but he remained, to the end of his life, a performer, declaiming poetry at the drop a hat, reading aloud to his family from the classics, and cultivating an unmistakably Pickwickian personality. As a young man Evelyn was irritated by his father's performances, calling him 'incorrigibly theatrical'. But as several of his friends attested, he was always an actor himself, capable, as Anthony Powell recalled, 'of completely carrying through any given role he had provisionally assumed'. For instance while on a wartime parachute course he dumbfounded his mess-mates, most of them very young men, by posing as a veteran of three previous wars: the Great War, the Boer War and even the Zulu War.

Arthur left Oxford with the coveted Newdigate Prize for Poetry and the ambition to earn a living by his pen. Writing came easily to him and he had an ally in his kinsman, the influ-ential critic and essayist Sir Edmund Gosse. Gosse persuaded the Brute to give Arthur an allowance of £100 a year until he could earn his keep. He introduced Arthur to famous friends of his like Henry James, Thomas Hardy and Robert Louis Stevenson, and brokered Arthur's first major commission, a life of Tennyson, published shortly after the Laureate's death, that became a bestseller.

Arthur met Catherine Raban, or 'K' as he called her, while still a boy at Sherborne School. He knew from the start that K was the girl for him; she was calm, practical and loyal – which was just as well, since it was not until October 1896, by which time he was thirty and she twenty-six, that they could afford to marry. Their first home was a flat above a dairy in the Finchley Road. Arthur now had a choice: continue as a freelance, or find a secure job in the literary world that would allow him to write in his spare time. He chose the latter, joining the publisher Kegan Paul as a reader and adviser. He and K moved to a small house in Hillfield Road, West Hampstead, not far from the boisterous district of Kilburn, with its large Irish community. It was there, in 1898, that Alec was born, followed five years later by Evelyn. By then Arthur had been appointed managing director of Dickens's old publisher, Chapman and Hall, a job he was to hold until 1929. A little later he began to review books for the *Daily Telegraph*, which he did for the rest of his life.

In 1906 the Brute died, leaving Arthur just enough money to realize the dream of building his own house. The result was Underhill, a three-storey suburban villa in North End Road, near Hampstead Heath. Arthur was proud of this unpretentious dwelling, but even as a small boy Evelyn much preferred his maiden aunts' atmospheric house in Midsomer Norton, virtually unchanged since the 1870s and full of the sort of ornamental Victorian bric-a-brac that in middle age he began to collect himself. To make matters worse, in 1908 the London Underground was extended to nearby Golders Green, which grew so rapidly that it soon enveloped Underhill. Much to his subsequent embarrassment, Evelyn became a resident of this upstart suburb.

Compared with Arthur, Evelyn had a cushy childhood – too cushy, he later admitted. He spent his early years watched over by two 'adored deities', his mother and his nurse, a kindly, God-fearing girl from Somerset called Lucy. But whereas Lucy gave him her undivided attention, K transferred her ministry to Arthur the moment he arrived home from work. Evelyn resented this, and he resented even more the favouritism shown to Alec, with whom his father, in particular, was besotted. But Alec was away for most of the year, initially at a prep school so spartan that everything that happened to him afterwards seemed, in comparison, 'tame'. Evelyn was spared this because Arthur doubted whether, in the event of a war, he could afford two sons at boarding school. So Evelyn remained at Heath Mount, the inexpensive and unpretentious day school he had entered aged seven.

But Arthur soon had more to worry about than school fees. His beloved Alec may have been the sort of boy for whom the public school system was designed, spouting poetry one minute and hitting the winning six the next, but he was also an adolescent, with an adolescent's 'urges'. The upshot was that to Arthur's chagrin, Alec left Sherborne a year early, under the proverbial cloud 'no bigger than a boy's hand'. His precocious response was to write a novel called *The Loom of Youth*, which affirmed that such clouds were an integral feature of the public-school firmament. It enjoyed a resounding *succès de scandale*, the fallout from which meant that Evelyn would not be welcome at Sherborne. Aware that the son in whom he had taken so little interest was religious, Arthur sent him to Lancing College, 'a small school of ecclesiastical temper' on a windswept spur of the South Downs.

Belatedly, then, Evelyn found himself living on the wrong side of the green baize door. Here there was neither love nor privacy (even the lavatories had no doors) – just hostility, deprivation and noise. After three years of war everything seemed to be either soiled or makeshift and the food, what there was of it, 'would have provoked mutiny in a mid-Victorian poor-house'. But half-starved or not, boys were still expected to work and play as keenly as in peacetime. Any slackness would invite the admonition, from masters too decrepit to qualify as cannon-fodder themselves, that they were letting down the men in the trenches – among them Alec, who was later captured in the big German offensive of March 1918. No wonder Evelyn described this as 'the most dismal period in history for an English schoolboy'.

And then, as suddenly as they had begun, the guns ceased. Returning to Lancing in 1919, Evelyn was conscious of a new and exhilarating broom. Among the young masters released from active service was J.F. Roxburgh, later the first headmaster of Stowe, a tall, dandyish figure, always immaculately dressed, who combined personal idiosyncrasy with a touch of the grand manner. Evelyn fell under his spell. He worshipped panache, and this Roxburgh had in spades.

To hear him declaiming: '*Nox est perpetua, una, dormienda*' or '*Toute une mer immense où fuyaient des galères*' ... Not, as my father read poetry with a subtle cadence, but like a great negro stamping out a tribal rhythm – was to set up reverberations in the adolescent head which a lifetime does not suffice to silence.

Evelyn never became one of Roxburgh's pets (he had the wrong looks, rococo rather than classical), but Roxburgh thought highly enough of him to predict that he would make his mark, though quite how he left open.

That Evelyn was a born writer, already possessing impressive gifts of expression, can be seen from the remarkable diaries he had begun to keep as a schoolboy. But at Lancing, despite winning prizes for literature and poetry, and editing the school magazine, he was more interested in drawing and lettering. Roxburgh was not his only mentor. He also served a brief but formative apprenticeship in calligraphy and manuscript illumination under Francis Crease, a fastidious, *fin de siècle* scribe in whose tastefully furnished digs near the school he spent many 'golden hours'. Though he and Crease later fell out, Evelyn continued to think of himself as primarily a draughtsman for several more years. If he was a born writer, he was also an instinctive aesthete.

Though Evelyn enjoyed none of the prestige that accrued to the school's bloods, he was treated with guarded respect by his intimates, who included the future historian Roger Fulford, Hugh Molson, later a Conservative peer, and Max Mallowan, the archaeologist who became Agatha Christie's second husband. They acknowledged his intellect, rejoiced in his deadpan wit, but were wary of his caustic tongue, already identified by K as his 'besetting sin'. Another intimidating feature that Evelyn possessed was his 'penetrating sharp blue eyes'. Confronted by these at their first meeting, the future gossip-columnist and MP Tom Driberg, eighteen months younger than Evelyn but a head taller, was briefly rendered speechless. Nearly fifty years later Kingsley Amis's second wife, the novelist Elizabeth Jane Howard, found them equally arresting: '[T]hey were marvelously alive, *seeing* eyes that sparkled with intelligence and perception. Even Kingsley, when he did his very funny impersonation of Waugh's face – with its apoplectic edge of congested rage – couldn't manage the eyes.'

Evelyn had arrived at Lancing with some idea of becoming a parson, which aspiration the school, with its majestic neo-Gothic chapel and strong Anglican tradition, did nothing to discourage. Evelyn delighted in the chapel till the end of his days; it was the first of many buildings whose praises he sang. But after exposure to the well-bred scepticism of Enlightenment savants like Gibbon he began to have doubts, and by the time he left Lancing had lost his faith, cutting chapel regularly during his last term. Like many of those who were just too young to have fought, he was caught up in what his contemporary, George Orwell, called 'a general revolt against orthodoxy and authority'. When, in November 1919, George V proposed that the anniversary of the Armistice should be marked by a two-minute silence, Evelyn described it in his diary as 'a disgusting idea of artificial reverence and sentimentality'. He was particularly scornful of the OTC and the 'Corps-maniacs' who took it seriously. Yet his 'Bolshevism' was 'limited'. There were privileges he coveted, like being able to work in the school library, and for these he would conform.

Evelyn may have dreamt of becoming an artist-craftsman, but his immediate goal was to read History at Oxford, his first sight of which, in August 1920, produced this effusive tribute: 'I have never seen anything so beautiful.' Arthur hoped Evelyn might win a scholarship to New College, where he himself had been, but Evelyn chose to try for Hertford, a lesser-known college in the same examination group. He knew he wasn't up to an award at New College, and in any case the Hertford scholarship was worth more. Eager to leave school as early as possible he worked harder than he'd ever done before and in December 1921 was rewarded with a scholarship worth £100 a year.

Evelyn signed off as editor of the school magazine with a piece comparing his generation, the young men of 1922, with their immediate predecessors, 'the men who marched away'. Forty years on he described it as 'a preposterous manifesto of disillusionment', and 'totally false as a prediction of my own future or that of my contemporaries'. It was certainly false in one respect, because he said his generation would be 'reticent' – hardly an appropriate adjective for Evelyn himself, or indeed for Harold Acton, Cyril Connolly, Graham Greene, Robert Byron, Claud Cockburn, Anthony Powell and Brian Howard – to name just a few of the movers and shakers whom he met at Oxford, that 'Kingdom of Cockayne'.

Oxford and After
1922–7

We've only one virginity to lose
And where we lost it there our hearts will be.
Rudyard Kipling

A caveat is necessary here. Like Paris in the Twenties, Oxford in the Twenties is the stuff of legend, an arcadia in which simpering young nobs sip Château d'Yquem to the sound of trumpets, their lives unclouded by the need to pay bills or pass exams. To say that Evelyn alone was responsible for this is a little unfair, since several of his contemporaries attested to the *douceur de vivre* of that time and that place. But it is thanks largely to *Brideshead Revisited*, particularly the beguiling television series it inspired, that this myth has become so potent. No doubt Oxford in the Twenties was 'very heaven' for a privileged few. But as Anthony Powell pointed out, undergraduates then, however precocious in other respects, were by today's standards physically, sexually and emotionally retarded. Many of them were spotty youths (one reason why roll-neck sweaters became so popular) who did not in the least resemble the series' male leads, Jeremy Irons and Anthony Andrews, two lean and sinewy 'matinée idols' in their early thirties. If, as he later admitted, Evelyn was remembering with advantages, he could not have foreseen the liberties that would be taken with his novel.

In January 1922, less than a month after leaving Lancing, Evelyn took up his place at Hertford, 'a respectable but rather dreary little college' in the shadow of its venerable neighbour, New College. Forty years on he claimed it was no handicap to arrive a term late because it encouraged him to look beyond Hertford for his friends; but to begin with, his ambition to 'taste everything Oxford could offer and consume as much as I could hold', fed on the place rather than the people. Nothing much had changed since his father's time. Bells still peeled over a city of beautiful, if somewhat sooty, stone buildings, set amidst meadows and waterways and harbouring a rich assortment of eccentrics, many of them in Holy Orders. There were plenty of bicycles (Evelyn learnt to ride one his first term), but very few cars. And very few women. Undergraduettes were not only rare, but heavily chaperoned. Consequently, as Cyril Connolly noted, 'men who liked women were apt to get sent down'.

This was not a risk that Evelyn would run. Aged eighteen, the product of a boys' public school, he was as wary of women as his immortal scapegrace, Captain Grimes. And like Grimes – though for a different reason – he carried a walking stick, 'as heavy as a rifle', bought while he was still at Lancing, and from which at Oxford he was practically inseparable until it was lost in some drunken escapade. Grimes needed his stick because he'd lost a leg; but in Evelyn's case it was an early example of the props that contributed to his act. He later blamed Oxford for instilling 'a lifelong desire to draw attention to oneself', but the evidence suggests that he was always going to do this. 'Why do you make so much noise?' asked an affronted Cyril Connolly when Evelyn was shouting his head off in the porch of Balliol. 'I shout because I am so poor,' answered Evelyn.

If Evelyn was poor it was because, like the hero of Connolly's novel *The Rock Pool*, his main exercise at Oxford was running up bills. He had expensive tastes in suits, shirts, shoes and books, all of which the Oxford tradesmen would supply on tick. He was also a very generous host. So although, as he himself admitted, his yearly allowance of about £350 (which included his scholarship) was a little more than the average, it was not nearly enough to meet his requirements. The tradesmen could be appeased by further orders; but once he exceeded his modest overdraft level the bank refused to honour his cheques. He earned small sums by writing for undergraduate magazines and by designing book jackets, magazine covers and bookplates. At one point he raised some cash by selling off the expensively bound books he had acquired. But all too often he had to cadge – from his mother, from Alec, and from his friends, among them Terence Greenidge, a very odd fish indeed.

Evelyn's social climbing is a matter of record. His relish for *outré* characters like Greenidge, with whom he remained on good terms all his life, is less remarked. A year ahead of Evelyn at Hertford, and variously described as loony, dotty, crazy and absolutely crackers, Greenidge combined mild kleptomania – he stole small items like keys and hairbrushes, which he then hid, magpie-like, in odd places – with what sounds like obsessive compulsive disorder: he could not abide litter, so his pockets were always stuffed full of rubbish picked up in the street. He and Evelyn hit it off immediately. They shared a passion for the cinema, and later collaborated on a bizarre homemade film called *The Scarlet Woman* about a plot by the Roman Catholic Dean of Balliol, F.F. 'Sligger' Urquhart (played by Evelyn), to suborn the future Edward VIII. They were also addicted to ragging. One of their targets was 'Sligger', beneath whose rooms at Balliol Evelyn was yelling when Connolly accosted him. Another was Evelyn's tutor at Hertford, C.R.M.F. Cruttwell, who must have wondered what he had done to deserve a pupil as vindictive as Evelyn.

A fellow of All Souls whose traumatic experiences on the Western Front had made of him a martinet, Cruttwell returned to Oxford determined to lick his pupils into shape. He expected scholars to earn their stripes, something Evelyn was not prepared to do. 'From the first,' he recalled, 'I regarded Oxford as a place to be enjoyed for itself, not as the preparation for some-thing else.' It didn't help that after Roxburgh, Cruttwell was, in Evelyn's eyes, so unprepossessing: he had 'the face of a petu-lant baby' and 'smoked a pipe that was usually attached to his blubber lips by a thread of slime'.[1] Soon he and Cruttwell could not bear to be in the same room together, leaving Evelyn free to enjoy himself without the need to write a weekly essay. Greenidge then mischievously theorised that Cruttwell, an acknowledged misogynist who barred women from his lectures, enjoyed sexual congress with dogs. He and Evelyn would bark outside his rooms, brandishing a stuffed dog that Greenidge had bought from a junk shop. Why they weren't disciplined is a mystery. But if Cruttwell thought he'd heard the last of Evelyn when he went down in 1924, he was mistaken. Evelyn christened a succession of his delinquent minor characters 'Cruttwell', only ceasing when Cruttwell, probably suffering from delayed post-traumatic stress, was committed to an asylum, where he died in 1941.

The greatest favour Greenidge did for Evelyn was introducing him to the Hypocrites' Club (so-called because their motto was *Ariston men hudor,* classical Greek for 'Water is best'), a rackety undergraduate dive that briefly became a byword for unbridled dissipation. It was here, and at the more sedate luncheon parties given by Harold Acton, whom he met in his second year, that Evelyn first glimpsed, through the bottom of a glass, the Promised Land beyond Golders Green. Drink agreed with him. He was frequently drunk, a roaring boy who at one point was banned from the Hypocrites for breaking up the furniture with his stick. Beer, as he later admitted, was his standard tipple, sometimes preceded by sherry and followed by port. Unlike Charles Ryder in *Brideshead Revisited*, his acquaintance with wine was limited to concoctions like mulled claret and Emu, the Australian Burgundy favoured by Arthur.

Evelyn's drinking companions were engaging, often erudite, self-assured and socially irresponsible. Dandyish in manner and dress, their iconoclasm was confined to art, which for a brief period in the Twenties got mixed up with life. Wit was highly prized; to be thought 'amusing' everyone's ambition. No wonder Evelyn made his mark. John Sutro, a wealthy and ebullient bon vivant who introduced Evelyn to plovers' eggs, recalled an exchange with a policeman outside the club. 'Evelyn went up to the policeman, pointed at me, and said, "Constable, I want to charge this gentleman with committing an indecent assault on me." And the policeman, who was used to undergraduates, said, "I'm sure you don't mean that, sir." "Very well," said Evelyn, "I want to give myself up for committing an indecent assault upon myself."'

Consensual groping, if not indecent assault, was commonplace at the Hypocrites, particularly after a crowd of 'wanton Etonians' led by Harold Acton and Brian Howard, both card-carrying homosexuals, infiltrated the club. Evelyn, who unlike Alec had kept his hands to himself at school, became an enthusiastic fellow-traveller. His first love was Richard Pares, a brilliant, mop-haired Wykehamist. But Pares had no head for drink, and on that rock their relationship foundered. Drink was no obstacle to his next love, Alastair Graham; indeed their appetite for a glass was the equal of their appetite for each other. For two years they were virtually inseparable, staying at each other's houses, going off on long pub-crawls and taking no thought for the morrow. At one point, much to the annoyance of his mother, a widow with plenty of attack who inspired Lady Circumference in *Decline and Fall*, Graham guaranteed Evelyn's overdraft. He also hand-printed, on a press bought from Leonard Woolf, Evelyn's essay on the Pre-Raphaelites, on the strength of which Evelyn's first book, a life of Dante Gabriel Rossetti, was commissioned.

Evelyn destroyed his Oxford diaries,[2] so it is difficult to explain how this good-natured but otherwise unexceptional young man stole his heart away. In *A Little Learning*, where Graham appears as 'Hamish Lennox', Evelyn wrote, 'I could not have fallen under an influence better designed to encourage my natural frivolity, dilettantism and dissipation or to expose as vulgar or futile any promptings I may have felt to worldly ambition.' Graham, from a wealthy background, could afford to shun ambition. He worked for a few years as an Honorary attaché in Athens and Cairo before retiring to Wales, aged thirty, when his mother died. By then Evelyn had the bit between his teeth. Their paths never crossed again. But in 1962, in a letter to Daphne Fielding about the Cavendish Hotel's cockney proprietress, Rosa Lewis,[3] to whom he'd been introduced by Graham, Evelyn described him as 'my closest chum once'.

A more positive influence on Evelyn at Oxford was Harold Acton, the most talked-about undergraduate of his day. The son of an Anglo-Florentine art collector and his American heiress wife, Acton embodied cosmopolitan cultural chic. He took the 'resolutely insular' Evelyn under his wing and introduced him to the work of modernist writers like T.S. Eliot, James Joyce and Gertrude Stein. Though Evelyn would later dismiss experimental writing as 'gibberish', in his twenties he welcomed it as a bracing alternative to the fusty Georgian tradition espoused by his father. When Acton pronounced his first attempt at a novel, *The Temple at Thatch*, 'too English for my exotic tastes', he promptly burnt it. He and Acton must have made a pretty pair when out together: Acton tall, pale, side-whiskered, his 'Oxford bags' flapping beside the tightly rolled umbrella he always carried; Evelyn short and pink in a suit of pale blue tweed plus-fours and armed with his cudgel-like stick. What they had in common, according to Evelyn, was '*gusto* ... a zest for the variety and absurdity of the life opening to us; a veneration for (not the same) artists, a scorn for the bogus'.

Evelyn, recalled Sir Harold in 1967, was an undergraduate of multiple moods and talents: 'Spontaneous, ebullient, vivacious, then silent, sullen, staring at the world with critical distaste. Barking at his tutorial bogey, swilling pints of ale, shouting nonsense rhymes in the street, then retiring like a monk to his cell to draw covers for novels slightly under the influence of Eric Gill, whose woodcuts he admired.' That Acton had lusted after Evelyn is clear from this passage in his *Memoirs*: 'I still see him as a prancing faun, thinly disguised by conventional apparel. His wide-apart eyes, always ready to be startled under raised eyebrows, the curved sensual lips, the hyacinthine locks of hair, I had seen in marble and bronze at Naples, in the Vatican museum, and on fountainheads all over Italy.' Alas for Acton, those wide-apart eyes were firmly fixed on Alastair Graham. He could expect 'homage and affection', but not love.

Though Evelyn did not enjoy Acton's *réclame* he was prominent enough to be on the radar of an arty freshman like Anthony Powell, who went up in 1923. Why then was he ignored by Maurice Bowra, the charismatic young don whose early protégés included Evelyn's contemporaries Kenneth Clark and Cyril Connolly? Bowra's biographer, Leslie Mitchell, explains it thus. Bowra, he says, was a virile homosexual who detested people camping it up; so when he saw Evelyn arm in arm with Acton, who flaunted his sexuality, he marked his card accordingly. But if Bowra's memoirs are to be believed he knew not only Acton, but the incorrigible Brian Howard as well – which doesn't square with Mitchell's claim that he avoided such people like the plague. Could it be that to begin with Bowra felt the same way about Evelyn as Evelyn did later about Dylan Thomas: 'There but for the Grace of God…'? Both were pugnacious little men whose quick wits and sharp tongues compensated for their lack of inches, about which they were sensitive. But whereas Bowra believed in hard work as an article of faith, Evelyn, at Oxford, thought it a waste of time. It was not until he pulled himself together and wrote *Decline and Fall* that Bowra courted him.

The louche company Evelyn kept was also disapproved of by Alec, resulting in a confrontation that inspired Cousin Jasper's grand remonstrance in *Brideshead Revisited*. But whereas Jasper washed his hands of Charles Ryder, Alec not only gave Evelyn the benefit of the doubt but later, when his brother fetched up in London, introduced him to the bohemian art-smart world to which he, as a professional novelist and man-about-town, belonged. Meanwhile, having failed to persuade Arthur that he would be better off studying art in Paris, Evelyn began belatedly to cram for his Finals. It did him no good. He took a bad Third and left Oxford £200 in debt. Three months later, sick at heart because Alistair Graham had gone to spend a long holiday with his sister in Kenya, he came of age and resolved to put aside childish things and live a life of 'sombre decency'. This resolution was promptly forgotten when he was invited to a party at Oxford, where Acton and Co. were still in residence. It was the first of many such parties he would attend. So began two dismal, dissipated, debt-ridden years during which, according to his diaries, he was often near the end of his tether.

Evelyn's problems were compounded by his reluctance to accept that he was a born writer. It didn't help that Arthur and Alec came into this category, or that the atmosphere at Underhill, a house he found increasingly oppressive, was 'entirely literary' and filled with 'paper and ink'. He still saw himself as an artist-craftsman, working with his hands rather than his head. To the astonishment of his friend Christopher Hollis he declared that he would give up drink if he really thought it interfered with his art.

This was nonsense. Enrolled at Heatherley's, a London art school, he soon grew as bored with life drawing as with the History syllabus at Oxford, kept later and later hours, and left after one term. There followed an abortive apprenticeship to a printer which cost Arthur £25, the arrival of a sheaf of bills he could not possibly pay, and the realization that he would have to earn a living. 'In those days,' he recalled, 'schoolmastering was to the educated classes what domestic service was to the uneducated classes. It was the one job open to those who had failed or got into disgrace.' In January 1925 he joined the staff of Arnold House, a 'depressingly well-conducted' prep school on the remote Denbighshire coast. It soon became apparent that he had no aptitude for teaching small boys. But before he left, which he did after two terms, he had acquired one priceless asset in the shape of a fellow teacher, Dick Young, alias 'Captain Grimes', the unrepentant pederast whom no amount of disgrace could cast down.

Did Evelyn, as he relates in *A Little Learning* but omits from his diaries, really try to drown himself off the beach beneath the school? Probably not. But comparing his situation with those of his Oxford friends, most of whom seemed to have the ball at their feet, he must have wondered what would become of him. To make matters worse he was suffering from unrequited love for a girl called Olivia Plunket Greene, who had supplanted Alistair Graham in his affections. Olivia was a 'Modern Girl', hard-drinking, jazz-loving, opinionated – and prepared to sleep with anyone who took her fancy, which Evelyn, sadly for him, did not. But because they moved in the same circles, and she enjoyed his company, Evelyn was reminded time and again of her inaccessibility. It was about now, too, that he first began to suffer from the insomnia that would plague him for the rest of his life.

Having failed to find a job in London he reluctantly returned to schoolmastering, this time at Aston Clinton, a small crammer in Buckinghamshire for 'backward peers', where Olivia's brother Richard was teaching. The salary was the same as at Arnold House – £160 a term – but the school's proximity to Oxford and London meant that opportunities to spend it were considerably greater. A typical entry in his diary reads like this: 'I am very vexed tonight because after a fairly late night yesterday and with a formidable pile of uncorrected essays and exercises I have allowed myself to be induced to go to a dance in Tring with Claud [Cockburn].' The gift of a motorbike from Richard Greene, who left after two terms to teach at Lancing, was a mixed blessing. He could reach Oxford under his own steam, but the university had changed: it was no longer enough to be amusing; you had to be rich as well. Probably this contributed to the 'social resentment' that Anthony Powell thought Evelyn never entirely lost.

Christopher Hollis alleged that Evelyn enjoyed caning the boys at Aston Clinton. But when, in his fifth term, he was sacked, it was not boys who were to blame but the school's matron, at whom he made a drunken pass. Feeling 'rather like a housemaid who has been caught stealing gloves' he once more returned to Underhill in disgrace. There was nothing for it, he wrote the following day, but 'to set about being a man of letters'. In fact Evelyn was to make one final attempt to evade his literary destiny, enrolling in October 1927 for a carpentry course at the Holborn Polytechnic. If successful he hoped to become a cabinet-maker, a trade his mother thought he would have been happier at than writing. But his Muse was not to be denied. The 'pleasant objects' he was destined to make were books, not furniture.

The Best and Worst of Times
1927–30

> Although experience is the best of all teachers, her fees
> come exceedingly high.
>
> *Dean Inge*

On one of his rackety jaunts to Oxford from Aston Clinton
Evelyn sprained his ankle so badly jumping out of a window that
he had to convalesce at Underhill. Lying on the sofa there
he became absorbed in reading about the Pre-Raphaelite
Brotherhood, whose art had long attracted him, and by the time
he was back on his feet had resolved to write a book about them
himself. Nothing came of this until Alastair Graham, who had
bought a small printing press, suggested Evelyn write something
for him. Evelyn dug out the notes he'd made and in less than a
week produced an essay on the Brotherhood that Graham
printed and Evelyn himself had bound. Now fate took a hand in
the shape of Anthony Powell, then learning the publishing trade
at Duckworth's.

Two years behind Evelyn at Oxford, Powell only got to know
him properly when they were both trying to find their feet in
London. Evelyn impressed him because, despite the many set-
backs he'd received since leaving Oxford, his self-confidence
seemed unimpaired. 'He took the line that he was an adventurer
… and that sooner or later the right opportunity would turn up.'
At one of their meetings Evelyn presented him with a copy of

his essay. Since he'd been tasked to trawl on Duckworth's behalf among his contemporaries, Powell arranged for Evelyn to meet his boss, Tom Balston. Evelyn supplied his essay by way of credentials, on the strength of which Balston, who was keen to publish a new biography of Dante Gabriel Rossetti to coincide with the centenary of his birth, commissioned him on the spot.

Balston's commission was opportune because no sooner did Evelyn sign the contract and pocket the £20 advance (which he spent 'in a week') than he was sacked from his latest job, as a probationary reporter on the *Daily Express*. Arthur gloomily predicted that the book would never be written, 'so I'll have to make good the £20'. For once he did his son a disservice. After a family holiday in France that culminated in a visit to a Marseilles brothel with Alec – probably his first experience of sex with a woman – Evelyn got cracking on *Rossetti* and finished it within six months, a remarkable achievement in the circumstances. Did writing about Rossetti and his arty-crafty chums account for his odd decision to do a carpentry course? It seems likely; though when Powell, attending evening classes in typography at Holborn Polytechnic, ran into him there, he invoked 'Tolstoy and all that' as an explanation. A month or so later, finding himself on the same Tube train as Evelyn, Powell was even more astonished to learn that he was getting married, a leap in the dark, particularly if, like Evelyn, you lived from hand to mouth, but consistent with his vision of himself as an adventurer.

Evelyn first met the Honourable Evelyn Gardner in April 1927. She and a friend, Lady Pansy Pakenham, had digs above a tobacconist's near Sloane Square, an unconventional arrangement for young women of their sort which was made possible by their both being of age and having small private incomes. She-Evelyn, as it seems easiest to call her, was the daughter of the late Lord Burghclere, a Liberal politician, and his formidable wife, Lady Winifred, sister of the Egyptologist Lord Carnavon. Slim, petite, snub-nosed and Eton-cropped, she looked, said Nancy Mitford, 'like a ravishing page-boy'. According to Alec she was the best sort of Modern Girl – emancipated, but not in the least brassy. Unlike Olivia she was not promiscuous. But such was her modish allure that several men had already pursued her, to some of whom she had been briefly engaged.

Neither Evelyn's diaries, which he may have edited, nor his letters, offer much evidence of his interest in She-Evelyn before they were engaged. Indeed to judge from the number of times he mentions Inez Holden, a pretty, witty young journalist he met on the *Express*, you might suppose it was her he fancied. Then he writes that on 12 December 1927, over dinner at the Ritz, he proposed to She-Evelyn. The following day she rang to say she had accepted him.

Evelyn was a stickler for ceremony and etiquette: 'He always liked to lay down the law about behaviour,' said Anthony Powell. So it is worth noting that his proposal was far from decorous. He suggested that they should marry and see 'how it goes', hardly the vote of confidence a girl might expect from her suitor. No wonder She-Evelyn wanted to sleep on it. But Pansy Pakenham, whose nous she respected, spoke up for Evelyn, and marriage would also remove the long shadow cast by her despotic mother. So the die was cast.

Lady Winifred went on the offensive: 'It never occurred to me that I wasn't a gentleman until Lady Burghclere pointed it out,' Evelyn recalled. Having seen off her daughter's previous suitors she was determined to thwart this indigent scribbler as well. She was ruthless and thorough, obtaining a lurid indictment from Evelyn's old enemy Cruttwell, and then through her Establishment connections, scuppering his efforts to get a job with the BBC. But bolstered by their friends, and by Arthur and Catherine, who adored She-Evelyn, the young couple stood firm. Six months later, bored with waiting for a bus to Dulwich Picture Gallery, they decided to buy a marriage licence instead. Next day, 27 June 1928, they were married at St Paul's, Portman Square. Harold Acton was best man; Robert Byron gave away the bride, and Alec and Pansy Pakenham were the witnesses. Their honeymoon was spent in the Abingdon Arms, Beckley, where Evelyn had not only worked on *Rossetti* but also the comic novel, provisionally entitled *Untoward Incidents*, that he had begun as light relief from the labour of biography.

So was Evelyn at last reconciled to his lot as a writer? Resigned to it would be more accurate. Now that he was married he needed a regular income and, as he later – rather facetiously – explained, writing 'was the only way a lazy and ill-educated man could make a decent living'. Despite the apparent ease with which he wrote – *Decline and Fall* (the new title for his comic novel) took him under a year – he found writing – particularly comic writing – very hard work compared with drawing. In January 1929, shortly before setting out on the Mediterranean cruise described in his first travel book, *Labels*, he told Patrick Balfour that he was planning to do enough sketches en route to hold an exhibition which, if successful, would allow him to abandon writing for drawing.

Although *Rossetti* was generally well received Evelyn admitted in a letter to Harold Acton that he was 'not proud of it', repeating this many years later when interviewed by Julian Jebb for *The Paris Review*. But he was certainly proud of *Decline and Fall* even though, as a publisher's son, he must have known that it sailed very close to the wind. Unfortunately word of this reached the pompous chairman of Duckworth's, Gerald Duckworth, whose brother George was married to Lady Burghclere's sister. Gerald sided with Lady Burghclere over her daughter's marriage, so imagine his displeasure when he learnt that *Decline and Fall* contained ribald passages that might well land its publisher in court. Conscious of the chairman looking over his shoulder, Balston applied too much blue pencil, causing Evelyn to reclaim the manuscript and submit it instead to his father's firm, Chapman and Hall. They also insisted on excisions, but not so many as had Duckworth's. These Evelyn assented to, leaving Balston to wring his hands for evermore. It was scant consolation that Duckworth's retained the option on Evelyn's non-fiction.

Despite a generous notice from Arnold Bennett, Middle England's most authoritative reviewer, and the news that Winston Churchill had chosen it for his personal Christmas present, *Decline and Fall* was not an immediate bestseller. But it put Evelyn on the map, where he was determined to remain. He grasped immediately that getting your novel reviewed was not enough; you had to get people talking about it – and, better still, about you. 'A fashionable wedding is worth a four-column review in the *TLS*,' he told his fellow novelist Henry Yorke (who wrote as Henry Green). In time he became an assiduous networker, throwing lunch parties at the Ritz to which he would invite gossip columnists like his old schoolmate Tom Driberg, 'William Hickey' of the *Express*. But for now his best means of keeping his profile high was through journalism. Fortunately he possessed the three most effective weapons in a freelancer's armoury: readability, versatility, and a first-class agent, A.D. Peters, who did his best to ensure that when editors wanted a piece on, say, the 'Younger Generation', a major preoccupation then, it was to Evelyn that they would turn.

Recalling how vulnerable the two Evelyns looked as they embarked upon married life, Alec Waugh, whose own first marriage had been annulled on the mortifying grounds of non-consummation, said he'd prayed for charitable tides. His prayers went unanswered. Not long after they had rented a flat in the then unfashionable district of Islington, She-Evelyn had such a nasty attack of German measles that they 'couldn't move for doctors and nurses'. In the days before antibiotics it could take weeks to recover fully from even a mild infection, and over Christmas she developed tonsillitis. The New Year was bitterly cold, to escape which Evelyn proposed that they sail round the Mediterranean on a tramp steamer, which he would then write up. But his resourceful agent Peters came up with a better plan:

a free cruise round the Med on a Norwegian liner in return for some publicity for the shipping company.

Since neither of them had much experience of Abroad the cruise promised to be an adventure. Instead it rapidly became an ordeal. Even before they boarded at Monte Carlo She-Evelyn had become feverish; her condition did not improve aboard ship, and when they reached Port Said she was diagnosed with double pneumonia, prompting Evelyn to send Pansy Pakenham a postcard saying that by the time she received it, She-Evelyn would probably be dead. The local hospital saved her life; but by now their ship was far away, money was short and Port Said, belying its louche reputation, was 'incredibly dull'. There followed two very expensive weeks of convalescence at a hotel near the Pyramids. Then, thanks to loans from friends and family, they managed to reach Malta where their cruise ship, on its second round trip, reappeared. Eventually, five months after leaving London, they arrived home to be greeted by bills of over £200.

Evelyn's sketch-book was empty, but he had brought back several thousand words of a new novel about 'bright young people'. Eager to get on with it, he retreated once more to the pub at Beckley, while She-Evelyn's friend Nancy Mitford went to keep her company in Islington. With hindsight this separation may have been unwise, but it was not just the 'clasping tares of domesticity' that Evelyn was trying to avoid. He knew that London held too many distractions of the very sort about which he was writing. What he didn't know – what he couldn't have known – was that his marriage was on the rocks.

The cause was someone Evelyn himself had enjoyed seeing before they went abroad, a debonair Old Etonian employed by the BBC called John Heygate. Anthony Powell, who became a close friend of Heygate's, described him as the 'ideal spare man' – tall, good-looking, well-informed and well turned out, with money of his own and a flat in South Kensington. She-Evelyn, who confessed to a shocked Nancy Mitford that she had never loved Evelyn and had only married him to get away from her mother, fell for Heygate and almost immediately went to bed with him. When she told Evelyn he said he was prepared to forgive her if she promised never to see Heygate again. They were briefly reconciled. But once Evelyn returned to Beckley his wife went back on her word. So in August 1929 Evelyn moved out of their flat, which was in She-Evelyn's name, and began divorce proceedings. He was utterly downcast. 'I did not believe it was possible to be so miserable and live,' he told Harold Acton.

She-Evelyn may have been the guilty party, but it seems clear that Evelyn, compared with the more experienced Heygate, was a big disappointment in bed. When the newly deflowered Nina, in *Vile Bodies*, says she'd 'rather go to my dentist any day', you can't help wondering whether Waugh was quoting his wife. In another passage, which he later deleted, Waugh wrote: – '[L]like so many people of their age and class, Adam and Nina were suffering from being sophisticated about sex before they were at all widely experienced.' Nor can it have helped that no sooner did they marry than She-Evelyn's health broke down. Those tides invoked by Alec Waugh were anything but charitable.

'He did not repine' was a favourite phrase of Evelyn's. But when She-Evelyn left him he did repine. Indeed Nancy Mitford, who transferred her affections from She-Evelyn to Evelyn, thought her defection was 'the clue to so *much*'. Nevertheless he bit the bullet and finished *Vile Bodies*, the comic novel, begun aboard ship, that became a bestseller and made his name. A better description would be 'serio-comic', since for every critic who said they'd laughed out loud there was another who identified the underlying despair. No doubt this was partly a reflection of Waugh's state of mind after his marriage broke up. But it is well to remember something he subsequently wrote – 'the artist is always and specially the creature of the Zeitgeist'; and what shaped his generation's imagination was *The Waste Land*, with its bleak vision of the post-war world.

Evelyn was lucky in one respect. The frivolous young world-lings he wrote about, with their crazes, their childish slang and their relentless partying, had not quite reached their sell-by date. But within eighteen months the country's mood had changed. Hunger marches had begun, millions of people were on the dole, and there was a steady run on the pound, culminating in a financial crisis. On 21 September 1931 Britain went off the Gold Standard, 'the biggest shock', according to Alec, 'that my generation and their predecessors had ever known'. Overnight the Roaring Twenties were silenced. It was time to sober up.

Before that, however, Evelyn had to convince readers that his pleasure cruise had been an unqualified success, and not the distressing prelude to heartbreak it undoubtedly was. He did so by posing as a discerning bachelor in search of local colour who befriends Geoffrey and Juliet, a young English couple whose trip nearly ends in tragedy when Juliet falls dangerously ill. Published in Britain as *Labels*, and in America, more accurately, as *A Bachelor Abroad*, it contains this characteristically booby-trapped purple passage:

> I do not think I shall ever forget the sight of Etna at sunset; the mountain almost invisible in a blur of pastel grey, glowing on the top and then repeating its shape, as though reflected, in a wisp of grey smoke, with the whole horizon behind radiant with pink light, fading gently into a grey pastel sky. Nothing I have seen in Art or Nature was quite so revolting.

But Evelyn was smart enough to realize that a little spleen went a long way in a travel book, pleasantly surprising one reviewer who had heard him described as 'the second most impertinent young man in London'. He was soon packing his bags again, to cover the Coronation of Haile Selassie in Addis Ababa. Included in his luggage was a Missal. To the dismay of his parents and the astonishment of most of his friends he had just been received into the Roman Catholic Church.

Religion had played no part in Evelyn's life since he lost his faith at Lancing. At Oxford, Hertford was one of the only colleges that did not require undergraduates to attend daily chapel, so he had not even been required to go through the motions. True, a couple of his close friends, Christopher Hollis and Alastair Graham, had subsequently 'Poped', but if he was influenced by this he chose not to advertise the fact. Most of the people he knew were 'fashionable agnostics'. And one of those to whom he turned for succour in the wake of She-Evelyn's defection was Maurice Bowra, a thoroughgoing pagan whose distaste for Catholicism, says his biographer, was 'deep and real'.

So why did Evelyn take the plunge? The most common assumption was that having been shattered by his wife's betrayal he needed a refuge and found it in the Catholic Church. Evelyn himself gave more than one explanation. At the time, he said it came down to a choice between (European) Civilization and Chaos. In the eighteenth century it was possible for a 'polite sceptic' like Gibbon to accept the benefits of civilization and at the same time deny the supernatural basis on which it rested. But the spread of a powerful materialistic creed like communism meant that our civilization must re-embrace Christianity in order to survive. And only the Catholic Church had the 'combative strength' to ensure that survival. Twenty years later he explained that as a young man he had concluded that 'life was unintelligible and unendurable without God'. And if Christ was the son of God – as a 'brilliant and holy priest' convinced him – then the church that his disciple Peter founded in Rome must be the true church. So 'on firm intellectual conviction but with little emotion' he became a Roman Catholic. Then in 1960, in a television interview, he said that even when he lost his faith he realized that to be a Christian was to be a Catholic. So his conversion, when it came, was to Christianity, rather than to Catholicism as such.

Like many converts Evelyn became, in Tom Driberg's words, 'more ultramontaine than the Pope'. He even went so far as to say that for him, 'Christianity began with the Counter-Reformation'. But the charge that we should 'live more nearly as we pray' did not come easily to him. He once asked Sir William Beveridge, architect of the Welfare State, how he got his main pleasure in life. 'By trying to leave the world a better place than I found it,' said Sir William.' 'And I get mine,' said Evelyn, 'in trying to spread alarm and despondency, and I expect I get a great deal more than you.' No doubt this was a tease, but it had a basis in fact. When, as often happened, his friends rebuked him for behaving in an un-Christian manner, he would simply reply, 'You have no idea how much nastier I would be if I was not a Catholic.' Support for this admission came from Hilaire Belloc, an equally militant Catholic with whom Evelyn was sometimes compared. After meeting Evelyn for the first time Belloc is said to have exclaimed, 'He is possessed.'[4]

Home and Abroad
1930–7

It's very hard to be a gentleman and a writer
W. Somerset Maugham

Not long after meeting his first wife, Evelyn admitted that his appetite for beery debauches had diminished, the first sign that he was preparing to board the social escalator. He was not alone in this. As Cyril Connolly recalled: 'To be accepted by the upper class, then in possession of money and authority and even glamour, was a natural ambition.' It was an ambition more easily achieved now that the Edwardian era had closed. Just as in London mansions were being demolished to make way for mansion flats, so Society gave way to café society. The great charm of the famous parties of the Twenties was that you might meet 'anyone' at them, meaning that some at least of the barriers erected by the *ancien régime* had come down. For a gifted few beneath the salt the chance to rise above it was there for the taking.

Evelyn had further to climb than most of his coevals. At Oxford, as is clear from the opening of *Decline and Fall*, he steered well clear of the oafish Bullingdon set. Nor, later on, did he receive invitations to debutante dances. Although very dapper – it was hard to imagine him without a tie – he did not really look the part: 'a bright-eyed, pink faced, reddish haired, stocky jawed, coarse lipped youth' was how Harold Nicolson described him in 1930. But he had grit, stamina, a facility for buffoonery (essential weapon in the arriviste's armoury, so Anthony Powell thought) and, above all, wit. This last is clear from his writing. But what we cannot grasp is how funny he could be off the cuff. John Sutro, himself a gifted mimic, said he possessed a 'continual bubbling humour that is very difficult to describe', while Lady Dorothy Lygon, recalling how he could turn 'the most unlikely situations into irresistibly funny jokes', said it was 'like having Puck as a member of the household.'

But Evelyn was not content to be a court jester. He wanted to get on equal terms with the quality, which meant, among other things, keeping up with them in pursuit of the fox. To do this he had to learn to ride, putting himself in the steely hands of Captain J.H. Hance, riding instructor to the gentry. Although he went at it with a will it was patently obvious, as he later admitted, that he was only there 'for social reasons'. The first time the young Wilfrid Sheed recalled hearing his name it provoked this withering put-down: 'Wasn't he that little pink chap who used to show off on the hunting field?'

Whatever social advantages Evelyn may or may not have gained from hunting, his lessons with Captain Hance had definite literary consequences. The captain's riding academy was in Malvern, the nearest town to Madresfield Court, ancestral home of the Lygon family whose head, Lord Beauchamp, known as 'Boom', had recently been driven into exile following a homosexual scandal. Evelyn had met Boom's two eldest sons at Oxford and probably had a brief affair with Hugh, the younger, a charming trifler with a weakness for drink who suffered, said his sisters, from 'second son syndrome'. It was thanks to two of these sisters, Lady Mary and Lady Dorothy, that Evelyn had the run of Madresfield, where they presided as joint *châtelaines* following their father's disgrace. Without this first-hand knowledge of country house living it's doubtful if he could have written either *A Handful of Dust* or *Brideshead Revisited*. Moreover, while Hugh was to some extent the model for Sebastian Flyte, there are also parallels between Boom's exile and that of Lord Marchmain.

As his playful letters to them show there was something of the schoolroom – or even the nursery – about Evelyn's relationship with the Lygon sisters. Some readers may think, as Anthony Powell did, that he was showing off, but there is no doubting that during the years when, as he put it, he had 'no fixed abode and no possessions which would not conveniently go on a porter's barrow', Madresfield was where he felt most at home. In the Lygon sisters' company he was at his most engaging, the comic genius who, for all his faults, could be the best company in the world. One day he and Mary were sitting by a fountain in the garden on which was inscribed the motto, 'The day is wasted on which we have not laughed.' 'Well,' said Mary, 'we haven't wasted many days, have we?'

But much as he loved Madresfield, Evelyn found it almost impossible to work there for long. The girls were very demanding and, 'lazy bugger' that he was, he could not refuse them. Luckily his friend Patrick Balfour, who heard about it from Alec, had found the perfect refuge: the Easton Court Hotel at Chagford, on the edge of Dartmoor, a comfortable, centrally-heated old farmhouse (now listed) whose American owner, Mrs Cobb, prided herself on 'understanding writers' ways'. With the exception of two months at a hotel in Fez, chosen because he wanted somewhere cheap and sunny, Chagford was where Evelyn did most of his serious writing until his marriage to Laura Herbert in 1937.

Soon after meeting the Lygon sisters Evelyn pulled off an even greater social coup. He got to know Lady Diana Cooper, an Edwardian society beauty, the pin-up of the Great War's brilliant 'Lost Generation', who had reinvented herself as an actress playing the Madonna in Max Reinhardt's smash-hit religious spectacle *The Miracle*. To begin with Evelyn made the mistake of pursuing her, unaware that unlike her predatory husband, the Tory MP Duff Cooper, she thought sex overrated. Once it became clear that she wanted him as a friend and not a suitor they established a bond that lasted until Evelyn's death, exchanging literally hundreds of letters and postcards. 'I wanted to bind him to me with hoops of steel,' recalled Lady Diana, the model for Mrs Algernon Stitch, whose shameless disregard for rules and regulations was, so Evelyn thought, consistent with the unshakeable self-assurance that went with high birth.

But those 'hoops of steel' were sometimes strained to breaking point, a persistent threat being the enmity between Evelyn and Duff Cooper. Much as she craved the attention of admirers like Evelyn, Lady Diana was devoted to her husband, whom she married in the teeth of opposition from her snobbish family. Evelyn was certainly envious of Duff, not simply because he was married to Diana, but because he was a genuine man of action, a role Evelyn coveted when young. It cannot have helped that in addition to the DSO he won in 1917 Cooper had published an acclaimed biography of Talleyrand, matching Evelyn at his own game. Diana herself was not blameless, either. Although she kept Evelyn at arm's length, she could not bear the thought of sharing him with another woman and was distinctly cool towards his future wife, Laura Herbert, who had the added disadvantage in her eyes of being the daughter of one of her oldest friends.

As an insular youth, Evelyn was dismissive of 'bloody abroad'. He changed his tune when it became apparent that there was a thriving market for intelligent travel books that might absolve him from writing pieces like 'My Favourite Film Star' and 'This Sunbathing Business'. 'We travelled as a matter of course,' he recalled – 'We' being clever, literate young men like him who didn't mind roughing it, particularly if, as he did, they got a novel out of their journey as well. So it was that his East African book, *Remote People,* which began in Abyssinia and ended in the Belgian Congo, provided much of the material for *Black Mischief;* while without the unsuccessful attempt he made to reach Manaos, described in *Ninety-Two Days*, there would have been no Mr Todd, the nightmarish Dickens fanatic who shackles Tony Last in *A Handful of Dust*.

But in a piece written for the *Daily Mail* Evelyn insisted that he didn't travel simply in order to write books about it. For a start, writers needed to get away from their desks or risk going off their heads. And if a little bit of hardship or even danger was involved, so much the better. Then again you could learn a lot about people – the novelist's stock in trade – by viewing them in unfamiliar surroundings. Finally there was sheer curiosity: what is that dot on the map really like?

Although he experienced a great deal of discomfort, Evelyn did not pretend to be an intrepid explorer in the Peter Fleming mould. 'The very stuff of travel,' he reckoned, was not the dramatic incidents, 'but the day to day routine … the delays and uncertainties, the minor vexations – whole drab, uneventful patches of sheer hard work and discontent.' You need look no further for confirmation of this than his account of running round and round in circles trying to obtain a medical certificate in the Belgian Congo. But however parlous his predicament, he had only to pour himself a drink and every prospect pleased. Alcohol, he reckoned, was the one essential requirement for foreign travel, 'whether cruising along the French Riviera in a yacht or ploughing through unmapped areas of virgin forest'.

Another of Evelyn's rogues, the globetrotting brigand Basil Seal, would surely have endorsed this. We meet him for the first time in *Black Mischief*:

He stood in the doorway, a glass of whiskey in one hand, looking insolently round the room, his head back, chin forward, shoulders rounded, dark hair over his forehead, contemptuous grey eyes over grey pouches, a proud rather childish mouth, a scar on one cheek.

'My word he is a corker,' remarked one of the girls.

Basil certainly has sex appeal, and the morals of a tomcat. Insolent, irresponsible and unscrupulous, he has made his way in the world through a combination of sophistry, low cunning and sheer nerve. With a little more application he might have achieved the great things once predicted of him, but application is not Basil's strong suit. Rather than score the winning goal he would prefer that the stadium went up in smoke. Bored with Mayfair, he steals his mother's emerald bracelet and decamps to the East African kingdom of Azania whose young, Oxford-educated Emperor makes him Minister of Modernization. In a country where the soldiers would rather eat their boots than wear them this is a challenging assignment. And Azanians eat people, too, so that when Basil tells his mistress he'd like to eat her, he has no idea that this is precisely what he will do.

Evelyn acknowledged that 'some readers' recognized in Basil a combination of two dissolute Oxford acquaintances of his, Peter Rodd – 'Prod' – who married Nancy Mitford, and Basil Murray, son of Gilbert Murray, the professor of Greek. But there is a lot of Evelyn too. As his friend Ann Fleming noted, Evelyn liked things to go wrong. If nothing else, mishaps were an infallible antidote to boredom, to avoid which he would go to almost any lengths. This nearly proved his undoing in July 1934, when after a dissipated interlude in London, he decided on the spur of the moment to go to Spitzbergen with Hugh Lygon, who now led an outdoor life, and a young friend of Hugh's called Sandy Glen. They were on a reconnaissance mission for an Arctic expedition planned the following year, but from the start everything went wrong. Unusually high temperatures turned the snow to slush, making progress with a loaded sledge penitential. Throughout Evelyn found it hard to keep up with the other two, who were in much better shape. Then he and Hugh were nearly swept away trying to cross an icy torrent. 'So this is it,' thought Evelyn, who described the jaunt to Tom Driberg as 'hell – a fiasco very narrowly retrieved from disaster'.

Evelyn used Driberg as his unofficial press agent. For instance, when he became a Catholic he saw to it that Driberg mentioned this in his column, thus relieving him of the chore of writing dozens of letters. He used Driberg again to respond to attacks made on him by Ernest Oldmeadow, editor of *The Tablet*, a Catholic weekly regarded as the mouthpiece of the Catholic Primate, Cardinal Bourne. When *Black Mischief* was published, Oldmeadow, without mentioning its title, said he was disgusted that someone professing to be a Catholic could have written such an obscene and blasphemous book. Evelyn responded with a long and magisterial letter to Cardinal Bourne defending himself against Oldmeadow's 'ignorant and ill-judged attack'. The Cardinal's response is unrecorded, but Oldmeadow had another go at Evelyn over *A Handful of Dust*, saying that the grisly fate ordained for the hero, Tony Last, showed a lack of compassion that was un-Catholic. Driberg reported this in his column, whereupon Evelyn counter-attacked with a letter that Driberg published the following day. He argued that while Oldmeadow could say what he liked about the novel on literary grounds, he had no business giving a moral lecture: 'Long employment by a Prince of the Church has tempted him to ape his superiors, and, naturally enough, he gives an uncouth and impudent performance.' In 1935 Cardinal Bourne died, and the following year *The Tablet* was bought by a consortium of Catholic businessmen, who installed an old friend of Evelyn's, Douglas Woodruff, as editor. For the next thirty years Evelyn was a regular contributor.

Evelyn would have known that Ernest Oldmeadow was by no means the only prominent Catholic to question his bonafides, so to coincide with the rebuilding of Campion Hall, the Jesuit study centre in Oxford, he put aside fiction and wrote a life of the man it was named for, the Jesuit martyr Edward Campion. Emphasizing that it was not a work of scholarship Evelyn said it should be read 'as a simple, perfectly true story of heroism and holiness'. As a young man Campion had enjoyed the patronage of Queen Elizabeth, whom Evelyn later described as 'the vilest of her sex'. Had he trimmed he would probably have died full of honours, acknowledged 'as one of the great masters of English prose'; but 'by the grace of God', the phrase Evelyn used in respect of his own conversion, he chose martyrdom in the service of 'the Eternal Church'.

Evelyn was very nervous about the reception of *Edmund Campion*, 'Just like a spinster with a first novel.' He need not have worried, for although his Oxford contemporary Peter Quennell might complain of its partiality – 'the Catholic point of view underlines every paragraph' – and there were huffings and puffings from militant Protestants, reviews were generally favourable, his spare and elegant prose being singled out for praise. Gratifyingly, *Campion* was awarded the prestigious Hawthornden Prize. Since Evelyn had already made over the proceeds of his book to Campion Hall – the first of many such gifts to Catholic institutions and charities – he did not benefit materially from the award. But it lent weight to the belief held by many of his peers that he was already, in Henry Yorke's words, 'the outstanding writer of our generation'.

Although Evelyn was always determined to be as orthodox a Catholic as possible, in early days there were certain sins he had no qualms about committing, one of them being fornication. At Fez, as he informed the Lygon sisters, he patronized one of the local brothels. In London he favoured a tart called Winnie, afterwards visiting the Jesuit church at Farm Street to be shriven. He also had affairs with married women, one of whom wrote him such an anguished letter following his marriage to Laura Herbert – 'my heart aches as if it were a stone cut by a diamond' – that the reader glimpses a side of him that was otherwise hidden. But Evelyn was a romantic: sex could never be more than a diversion for him. What he wanted was a wife and family, which by becoming a Catholic he had apparently forfeited, since his church did not accept divorce. Then, when he had fallen in love with a devout Catholic called Teresa Jungman, he learnt that if he could prove that neither he nor his wife had ever intended to take their marriage vows seriously, it might be possible to obtain an annulment that would leave him free to marry again. To do this he needed She-Evelyn to testify with him before an ecclesiastical court.

Considering that Mrs Heygate, as she now was, must have known how low in his estimation she stood with Evelyn, it is a tribute to her unselfishness that she agreed to appear before the court with him, having been coached in her responses beforehand. To his relief the court accepted Evelyn's plea; it only remained for the Vatican to confirm their decision, usually a formality, so Evelyn felt able to pop the question immediately. Ironically it turned out that like Olivia Plunket Greene, Teresa Jungman was not physically attracted to Evelyn. But long after she had turned him down Evelyn had not heard back from Rome. Eventually it transpired that the papers were still gathering dust in Westminster. They were then sent off but had to take their place in the queue, so that it was not until July 1936, nearly three years after the hearing, that the annulment was finally granted.

The conclusion of *Black Mischief*, which takes place soon after Britain went off the Gold Standard, has Basil Seal back in London and rejecting the chance to go to a party, prompting one of his unregenerate friends to wonder if, like everyone else, 'Basil isn't going to turn serious on us too.' And what about Evelyn? Well, he was still up for parties, work permitting, but his new novel, considered by many to be his finest, was an indictment of the way we lived then – 'we' being the sort of 'smartistic' metropolitan world he aspired to join when he married Evelyn Gardner. The title comes from *The Waste Land*: 'I will show you fear in a handful of dust.' The theme is adultery and its baleful consequences. The hero, Tony Last, is a nice dull man whose shallow, worldly wife Brenda, bored with life in the hideous sham-Gothic pile that is Tony's pride and joy, falls for someone she knows to be worthless but cannot give up. Matters come to a head when their son, named John like Brenda's lover, is killed in a hunting accident. Brenda thinks at first that her lover has died and exclaims 'Oh, thank God' when she learns it's her son. Tony, unaware of Brenda's chilling Freudian slip, nobly agrees to give her a divorce, a quixotic concession whose transparency is underlined when the tart he's hired insists on bringing her pert little daughter to Brighton with them for their dirty weekend. Then Brenda overplays her hand by demanding too much alimony. Tony, determined not to lose his house as well as his son, halts the divorce proceedings and decamps to South America in search of a Lost City. This proves as illusory as the trust he had reposed in Brenda. We leave him deep in the jungle at the mercy of Mr Todd, an illiterate madman who makes him read aloud the works of Dickens.

Evelyn said the novel began as unfinished business. He'd written a short story called *The Man Who Liked Dickens* about someone trapped in the jungle like Tony Last. But how had he got there? 'Eventually the thing grew into a study of other sorts of savages at home and the civilized man's helpless plight among them.' The savages include another of Evelyn's prize rogues, Mrs Beaver, the mother of Brenda's lover, a rapacious decorator modelled on Somerset Maugham's wife, Syrie (referred to as 'Farter' by Evelyn in a letter). Mrs Beaver makes a good living out of doing up what E.M. Forster called 'immorality flats' (Brenda takes one); but her forte is desecrating country houses like Tony's. Evelyn saw her as barbaric, yet he could not help investing her with the chutzpah he so admired in friends of his like Lady Diana Cooper. She is a much more vital character than her futile son John, who not only shares his name with Brenda's son, but also with She-Evelyn's lover, Heygate. Evelyn never publicly conceded that his own divorce furnished material for this novel, and the circumstances are quite different. But given that he was as gob-smacked by She-Evelyn's defection as Tony is by Brenda's it is natural to assume that he was getting his own back. Two years later a contrite Heygate wrote asking for

Evelyn's forgiveness and received in reply a postcard on which was written 'O.K. E.W.' But despite her evidence on his behalf at the ecclesiastical court he seems never to have forgiven his first wife. She must surely be the model for Millicent in his short story, *On Guard*, about a girl with a beguiling 'urchin's' nose which her jealous dog disfigures, dooming her to spinsterhood.

When Evelyn was in London he generally preferred to stay at his West End club, the Savile, rather than with his parents, who in 1933 sold Underhill and moved to a two-storey maisonette in Highgate village, a more salubrious district than Golders Green, but still a world away from Mayfair and Belgravia. Arthur Waugh, thought Alec, had never been happier. Relieved of his responsibilities at Chapman and Hall, though still retained as a consultant, his time was his own: he could read, write, watch cricket, walk the dog, doze off over the crossword. But Alec omitted one incident that must have devastated him. On a rare visit Evelyn managed to set alight Arthur's cherished bookroom with its hundreds of inscribed copies, 'thus destroying the carefully garnered fruits of a lifetime of literary friendships.'. Evelyn shrugged off this disaster in a light-hearted piece about his efforts to escape his literary destiny; if he felt much remorse it is not apparent. He continued to bear a grudge against his father over his preference for Alec. It cannot have escaped Arthur's notice that it is Dickens, his favourite author, who Tony Last must read aloud until he drops.

Dickens had once been a favourite of Evelyn's, too, and although he came to think of him as a hypocrite and 'a thumping cad', he acknowledged his 'magnetism'. Growing up in a house full of books before radio and television he read the nineteenth-century canon as a matter of course. But literature for him was never the 'sanctuary against adversities' that it was for Arthur, or indeed Alec, who said that for most of his life he had devoted a portion of each day to reading poetry. He confessed to John Betjeman that for years he 'didn't dare admit' that he couldn't get through Proust[5] and revealed in his diary that until he went to Hollywood he'd never heard of Scott Fitzgerald. Americans were amazed at his admiration for Erle Stanley Gardner, author of the Perry Mason mysteries. But the writer to whom he awarded the palm was P.G. Wodehouse, because, as he informed his friend Frances Donaldson, 'One has to admire a man as a Master who can produce on average three uniquely brilliant and entirely original similes to every page.'

Evelyn marvelled at the 'exquisite felicity' of Wodehouse's prose style and wondered if it weren't 'an inexplicable gift, like Nijinsky's famous levitations'. It is tempting to ask the same of his own prose, which had, said Graham Greene, the 'limpidity' of the Mediterranean before it was polluted by tourism. The common factor was a Classical education, in Wodehouse's case at Dulwich College, where another master of the simile, Raymond Chandler, was also educated. Though Evelyn described his own grasp of Latin and Greek as 'superficial', he did not think the hours devoted to learning them were wasted because one learnt 'that words have basic inalienable meanings, departure from which is either conscious metaphor or inexcusable vulgarity... The old fashioned test of an English sentence – will it translate? – still stands after we have lost the trick of translation.' Anyone denied this apprenticeship – 'most Americans and most women' – would always be at a disadvantage.

But Evelyn made an exception in the case of Ernest Hemingway. Reading Hemingway's first novel, *The Sun Also Rises* (called *Fiesta* in Britain), he learnt a lot from the way Hemingway made drunk people talk. This was important because although Evelyn's milieu was not Hemingway's, both were full of people who drank deep and often. Even his sober characters, said Evelyn, could surprise him by turning to drink. It seems almost superfluous to note that he and Hemingway were as fond of the bottle as the people they wrote about. When Evelyn, newly arrived at Oxford, was exhorting Tom Driberg 'to take to drink [because] there is nothing like the aesthetic pleasure of being drunk', Hemingway was declaring, 'I love getting drunk. Right from the start it is the best feeling.' In the end drink stifled them both, but long before that they had become imprisoned in their own fantasies, the difference being that whereas Hemingway never ceased to regard himself as a man of action, to the detriment not just of his art, but his sanity, Evelyn was cured of adventuring by the war. The role he then assumed, that of a country gentleman, while equally bogus, was not incompatible with his métier (though J.B. Priestley thought otherwise).

Unlike the nobs he mixed with Evelyn had no private income. Neither did he have any assets besides his pen and the money he could earn from it. In 1935, having made a present of *Campion* to his church, and with no new novel planned, he needed work. Then a crisis occurred in Africa that was made to order for him. Mussolini, desperate to expand Italy's meagre colonial empire, was threatening to invade Abyssinia, which Evelyn knew at first hand from his coverage of Haile Selassie's coronation. But whereas most educated opinion in Britain supported Haile Selassie, Evelyn thought Abyssinia a barbarous country that would benefit from Mussolini's 'civilizing mission'. Fortunately for him one of the few papers in Fleet Street to take a pro-Italian line, the *Daily Mail*, had just lost its leading foreign correspondent, so Peters, with a little help from Lady Diana Cooper, who knew the *Mail*'s owner, Lord Rothermere, was able to line up Evelyn in his place. Peters also brokered a very lucrative book deal with Evelyn's friend and fellow Catholic Tom Burns, who had moved from Sheed and Ward, the publishers of *Campion*, to the larger firm of Longman's.

To the disgust of the explorer Wilfred Thesiger, who was there as honorary attaché to the Duke of Gloucester, Evelyn had covered Haile Selassie's coronation wearing grey suede shoes, a floppy bow tie and Oxford bags. He did not make the same mistake this time, getting comprehensively kitted out at the *Mail*'s expense. But what he really needed was a reporter's nose.

His novelist's eye, which paid off when he came to write *Scoop*, cut no ice with his employers in Fleet Street, who grew increasingly impatient at his failure to follow up any leads. In fairness there were not many leads to follow up, because the Italian invasion had yet to take place. By chance Evelyn got wind of when it might begin, and, to put one over his rivals, cabled the news in Latin. But no one at the *Mail* knew Latin, so his dispatch was spiked. This can only have deepened his contempt for journalists, something the young Bill Deedes, on his first foreign assignment, strongly resented. When, in October, the war did start the Abyssinians kept the press corps well away from the front, a recipe for professional mayhem. 'The heaviest fighting,' Evelyn told Diana Cooper, 'is among the journalists.' He himself had a drunken brawl with one of the Americans. 'Only a shit could be good on this particular job,' he concluded.

By November the *Mail* had lost patience with Evelyn and, in December, he began a leisurely journey home via the Holy Land, buoyed up at the prospect of spending Christmas 'without the Hitlerite adjuncts of yule logs and reindeer and Santa Claus and conifers'. The next month he was granted an interview with Mussolini, on condition that he didn't write it up. Like many British conservatives, including Churchill, he was taken in by Mussolini, reckoning that he would thwart any attempts by Hitler to coerce Austria into the Reich. Their meeting went smoothly, despite Evelyn's accurate prediction that while the Italians might win a military victory, they could anticipate a long guerrilla war. Back home he began work on *Waugh in Abyssinia*, the punning title Tom Burns preferred to Evelyn's suggestion, *A Disappointing War*. But when, in May 1936, Addis Ababa fell and Haile Selassie went into exile, it was clear that he would have to return to round the story off. This he did in August, being made much of by the Italians, anxious to publish abroad their good intentions. Despite grumbling about 'exultant fascists', Evelyn endorsed the draconian rule imposed by the viceroy, Marshal Graziani, 'an amiable Christian gentleman'. He was particularly enthusiastic about the road-building programme: 'A main road in England is a foul and destructive thing, carrying the ravages of barbarism into a civilized land – noise, smell, abominable architecture and inglorious dangers. Here in Africa it brings order and fertility.'

As stated above, most 'common readers' deplored Mussolini's rape of Abyssinia, particularly when details of his armies' atrocities were published. But this was not the only reason why, except in Catholic circles, *Waugh in Abyssinia* was noticed unfavourably, if at all, when it was published in December 1936. The previous July another 'Christian gentleman', General Francisco Franco, had launched an insurrection against the Spanish government. Immediately the Spanish Civil War, and the siege of Madrid that began soon afterwards, swept the board as far as foreign news went. Meanwhile at home the Abdication Crisis came to a head. Little wonder that there was scant interest in a remote colonial war that was over and done with.

In August 1933, shortly before Teresa Jungman turned him down, Evelyn had spent a few days at a villa in Portofino owned by the Herbert family, wealthy West Country gentry who had recently become Roman Catholics. It was a boisterous house-party and Evelyn scarcely noticed Laura, the reserved 'white mouse' of seventeen who would become his second wife. But eighteen months later he told Mary Lygon that he had taken 'a *great* fancy to a young lady called Laura [with] a long thin nose and skin as thin as bromo'. She was quite unlike the worldly women he was accustomed to mix with and in the letter of proposal he wrote to her he was astute enough to eschew affectation and simply put his cards on the table. 'I have always tried to be nice to you and you may have got it into your head that I am nice really, but that is all rot. It is only to you and for you. I am jealous and impatient – but there is no point in going into a whole list of my vices. You are a critical girl and I've no doubt that you know them all and a great many I don't know myself.' Perhaps recalling that there were those who thought he had been unwise to abandon She-Evelyn in order to write, he also warned her what being married to a writer would entail: 'For several months each year we should have to separate or you would have to share some very lonely place with me.' Laura's reply has been lost, but presumably she gave him grounds for hope because in a later letter he thanks her for 'loving' him.

When he set out his stall Evelyn was still waiting to hear whether his annulment had been granted. And there was a further complication in that Laura was a first cousin of his first wife, prompting an elderly aunt to complain, 'I thought we'd heard the last of that young man.' Laura's mother Mary[6] was not happy either. She could see the point of Evelyn but had an aristocratic disdain for parvenus. To his credit Evelyn stood his ground. He might envy nobs their self-assurance but was proud of having got where he had through merit rather than the accident of birth. Had Laura wavered all might have been lost, but she and Evelyn presented a united front against which Mary Herbert could not prevail. In January 1937, six months after his annulment had been granted, Evelyn leaked the news of his engagement to Tom Driberg, requesting that no mention be made of his previous marriage, 'which by now most people have forgotten'. He and Laura were married in London on 17 April 1937. Their wedding presents included a large cheque from Alec's wealthy second wife Joan towards the cost of their honeymoon, which was mostly spent in Portofino. The day they arrived Evelyn wrote in his diary, 'Lovely day, lovely house, lovely wife, great happiness.'

Borrowed Time
1937–40

Civilisation is a luxury which must be fought for.
Cyril Connolly

Now that he was married Evelyn's roving days were over, he hoped, for good. He wanted the settled, patriarchal life of a country gentleman, with a large household, a pleasant park and a well-stocked library and cellar. All of this would be costly, and as usual he was heavily in debt. Fortunately Joan Waugh's was not the only large cheque he and Laura received. Laura's grandmother, Lady de Vesci, gave them £4,000, with which they bought Piers Court, a handsome but very dilapidated eighteenth-century manor house near Dursley, on the edge of the Cotswolds. The roof leaked and there was no electricity or gas, but the house came with forty acres, assorted cottages and a view across Berkeley Vale to the Severn estuary and the Black Mountains. Not that Evelyn got any pleasure from natural beauty. He was more intrigued by the thought that Berkeley Castle was where Edward the Second met his gruesome end.

Once Piers Court became habitable, Evelyn, as assured in his taste as Mrs Beaver, directed the refurbishment. This included displaying the Waugh coat of arms, the validity of which he established with the College of Heralds, within Piers Court's pediment beside that of his wife. His aim, said Penelope Betjeman, 'was to give the impression of a country house lived in by the same family for several generations' (which had in fact been the case: a family called Pynffold lived there throughout the seventeenth and eighteenth centuries). One refinement he did not consider worth the expense was central heating. Underhill had been a cold house and Piers Court would be the same. Though he later did his best to escape the worst of the English winter Evelyn could not abide overheated rooms and was once evicted from a hotel in New Orleans when he tried to break a window that wouldn't open.

Laura, meanwhile, was experiencing the first of her many pregnancies, so it was lucky that Evelyn's new novel, *Scoop* (1938), in which Mrs Stitch appears, was his most successful yet, a comic *tour de force*. It turns on a case of mistaken identity. Lord Copper, the hardboiled owner of the *Daily Beast*, is persuaded by Mrs Stitch to send her protégé, John Boot, a modish young novelist like Evelyn, to cover the 'very promising little war' that's brewing in the African state of Ishmaelia. But wires get crossed and Boot's reclusive country cousin, William, who writes a nature column for the *Beast*, is sent instead. So the international press corps and its antics are seen through the goggling eyes of an innocent abroad. William is popularly supposed to have been based on Evelyn's Abyssinian war colleague, Bill Deedes, later the editor of the *Daily Telegraph*, a rumour Deedes did not discourage. But apart from the huge amount of kit they both cart round, the two men have nothing in common. Deedes was always 'Bill', never William. And although this was his first foreign assignment, he had been in Fleet Street for four years. If Evelyn did have him in mind he never mentioned it.

But Diana Cooper had every right to see herself as Mrs Stitch. 'Made a very good start on the first page of a novel describing Diana's early morning,' wrote Evelyn in October 1936. Like Captain Grimes, the ruthless, dynamic, alluring Mrs Stitch is a life force. Unlike Grimes, she rises again. It was 'madness' to kill off your characters, Evelyn later admitted, citing

P.G. Wodehouse and Anthony Powell as writers who had been clever enough to resist that particular temptation. The other 'immortal' in *Scoop* is Lord Copper, forever associated with 'Up to a point, Lord Copper', the nearest to a contradiction his foreign editor dares to utter. Lord Copper owes something to Evelyn's erstwhile employer, the autocratic Lord Beaverbrook, though not as much as the 'Byzantine vestibule' of Copper House does to the black glass *Express* building in Fleet Street. Beaverbrook was at home in the *beau monde*, Lord Copper is not, hence his capitulation to Mrs Stitch.

The civil war in Ishmaelia, like that in Spain, is between communists and fascists, allowing Evelyn to mock both 'isms'. So where did he stand on Spain? In 1937 leading authors in the democracies were asked which side they were on: that of the legally elected government of Spain, the Republicans, or the fascist insurgents under Franco, the Nationalists. Evelyn replied that he was no more impressed by the 'legality' of the Spanish government than were English communists by the legality of the Crown, Lords and Commons. Then: 'If I were a Spaniard I should be fighting for General Franco. As an Englishman I am not in the predicament of choosing between two evils. I am not a Fascist nor shall I become one unless it were the only alternative to Marxism. It is mischievous to suggest that such a choice is imminent.'

Given that Franco was seen as the Defender of the Faith, and that Laura's sister Gabriel was driving an ambulance for the Nationalists, the Catholic hierarchy might have expected a more ringing endorsement from the author of *Campion*. But Evelyn had good reason to be cautious. He earned his corn as a novelist, not as an apologist. Some of his readers must have winced at his support for Mussolini. It would have been folly to antagonise them further by becoming a cheerleader for Franco as well, whom in any case he seems not to have cared for. It is also worth remembering that for much of the war in Spain Evelyn was busy revisiting Abyssinia, getting married, finding and renovating

Piers Court and finishing *Scoop*, which he had begun two years before.

But Evelyn was not afraid to rebuke left-wingers like W.H. Auden and his circle who he thought had 'ganged up and captured the decade'. In a letter to the *New Statesman* he objected to their 'indiscriminate' and 'stultifying' use of the word 'fascist', comparing it to the way 'bolshie' was used in the Twenties. In both cases it became an all purpose epithet for 'anything or anyone of whom the speaker disapproved'. He returned to this theme in a review of Cyril Connolly's *Enemies of Promise*, some of which was written after Connolly had made common cause with the Auden group. Indignant that a good-timer like himself should have apostatized, Evelyn argued that 'fear of fascism' was a far more 'insidious' enemy of promise than those identified by Connolly. It was most unlikely that England would become fascist; 'but if anything is calculated to provoke the development which none desire, and Mr Connolly dreads almost neurotically, it is the behaviour of his hysterical young friends in the Communist Party'.

A book could be written on Evelyn's long and precarious friendship with Connolly, concluding with an incident after Evelyn's death when Connolly, reading an annotated copy of his *Unquiet Grave* in the Waugh collection at Austin, Texas, was so mortified by Evelyn's caustic *adversaria* – 'Look how he pursues me from beyond the grave!' – that he went home and sold all his cherished Waugh first editions.

Evelyn enjoyed teasing 'Boots' – short for 'Smartyboots', the epithet bestowed on Connolly by Virginia Woolf – deploying the same tactics against him as against Cruttwell. In *Black Mischief* there is an uncouth mercenary called General Connolly; in *Put Out Out More Flags* the feral evacuee children Basil Seal exploits are also called Connolly. And Connolly was not convinced by Evelyn's protestations that only an 'ass' would confuse him with a character in *Unconditional Surrender* called Everard Spruce, the libidinous, self-indulgent editor of a highbrow wartime magazine called *Survival* ('I nearly wrote, "Yours ever, Everard"', admitted Connolly in his PS to a letter on the subject). 'It is sad that Evelyn has such an urge to torture Cyril,' said Maurice Bowra. 'It must be a form of love.' Christopher Sykes was more charitable. He said that what Evelyn felt for Connolly amounted almost to 'amorous infatuation', and it is clear that one of the reasons Evelyn seconded Connolly's application to join White's was because he delighted in his talk, which could be as diverting as his own.

They had a great deal in common: presence; wit; snobbery (late in life Connolly boasted that every degree of the peerage had been represented at his son's christening); gluttony; bibliomania; sloth; self pity; and an insatiable appetite for gossip. 'Tell me some bad news,' Connolly would say. Evelyn, as his diaries and letters confirm, was the same. But whereas Connolly was wary of retailing the gossip he heard, particularly if it involved the misfortunes of friends, lest it became *his* turn next, Evelyn had no such qualms. 'I do not see how you can bear to go much into society if you feel this,' he told Connolly. So it is odd to learn that Evelyn said of Connolly what he said of Dylan Thomas, 'There but for the grace of God, literally ...' This may have encouraged the rumour that Evelyn had been assigned the task of enticing Connolly into the Catholic church. When Connolly heard this he said there was no chance of his 'going over' because it would mean that he could never look Maurice Bowra in the face again. In fact, as Evelyn himself knew, he was by temperament and conviction as unrepentant a pagan as Bowra and therefore beyond redemption. He was also, as Anthony Powell put it, 'one of those individuals – a recognized genius – who seem to have been sent into the world to be talked about'. The same applies to Evelyn. It is the most significant characteristic they shared.

But unlike Connolly, Evelyn did not put writing on a pedestal. He thought 'far higher gifts' were needed to paint even a bad picture than write a good book. He described writing as 'a trade' and saw writers as artisans, working with words to create and conceive a structure. What he admired about Somerset Maugham, an irretrievably third rate author in the eyes of many of his contemporaries, was his technique. Reading him, he had 'the same delight as in watching a first-class cabinet-maker cutting dovetails'. Maugham, he believed, was 'the only living studio-master under whom one can study with profit'.

In March 1938 Laura gave birth to a daughter, Teresa, described by Evelyn as 'huge and loud'. Two months later he reported to Peters that 'a very rich chap' was prepared to pay him to write a book about Mexico. The very rich chap was the Honourable Clive Pearson, and he had an axe to grind. In Mexico the huge concerns owned by his family had been confiscated by the left-wing government of General Lázaro Cárdenas. Since most people's eyes were fixed firmly on Europe this piracy, as Pearson saw it, passed virtually unnoticed except on the left, where it was greeted with approval. Pearson was offering about £1,000 up front, plus generous expenses, for Evelyn to indict Cárdenas. An added inducement from Evelyn's point of view was that for several years the Catholic church in Mexico had been persecuted, so he would be able to draw attention to its sufferings as well.

Laura, unencumbered by Teresa, accompanied Evelyn on this jaunt. She must have contributed to the fiction that he was there as a tourist, not an investigator hired by the Pearsons. He saw and heard enough to make a case against the regime, but framing it proved a chore – like composing 'an interminable *Times* leader of 1880' he told Diana Cooper. Entitled *Robbery Under Law* it was published in June 1939, an inauspicious date for a book about Central America. Hitler had entered Prague in March and it was clear that Europe was living on borrowed time. Another disadvantage was that Graham Greene had beaten Evelyn to the punch with *The Lawless Roads*, his strident attack on Mexican anti-clericalism and corruption. There remains, however, one redeeming feature of an otherwise superfluous book: a long passage in which Evelyn defines what being a conservative entails for him. At its core are three principles it was then deeply unfashionable to affirm:

> I believe that inequalities of wealth and position are inevitable and that it is therefore meaningless to discuss the advantages of their elimination; that men naturally arrange themselves in a system of classes; that such a system is necessary for any form of cooperative work, more particularly the work of keeping a nation together... I do not think that British prosperity must necessarily be inimical to anyone else, but if, on occasions, it is, I want Britain to prosper and not her rivals... I believe that Art is a natural function of man; it so happens that most of the greatest art has appeared under systems of political tyranny, but I do not think it has a connection with any particular system, least of all with representative government, as nowadays in England, America and France it seems popular to believe...

Evelyn also opined that 'war and conquest' were inevitable, but apart from unsuccessfully applying to join the Yeomanry – he was too old, they said – he carried on that summer as if it were business as usual, writing in the morning, gardening in the afternoon and, unlike everybody else, eschewing the radio, a device he abhorred. He had begun a 'spiffing' new novel and was also contemplating a history of the Jesuits for Tom Burns. Then, as the clock ran down, he suddenly changed tack and began firing off letters to anyone he thought could get him into the war. He was not alone. Thousands of other men who had been just too young to fight in the previous war were eager to do their bit in the next. But unless their qualifications for discomfiting the King's enemies were unassailable they, like Evelyn, found themselves 'on a list'.

Evelyn's motives were mixed. Although he believed the cause was a just one, particularly now that Stalin was Hitler's pal, he was also aware that a spell of active service would be a good career move. But it really must be 'active'. In his unpublished essay, *Writers at War*, he said it was 'the writer's function to aim at the heart of the matter and in war that lies at the extremity of the vast conveyor belt that puts the soldier into action, at the little ridge at the end of his sights…' Like John Plant, in the postscript to *Work Suspended*, he probably had in mind some 'plain regimental soldiering'. But it soon became apparent that the most likely form of 'National Service' for a portly, short-sighted writer in his mid-thirties was a desk job – 'the great uniformed bureaucracy' – which may be why, in a rash moment, he actually contemplated joining up as a private soldier, the drastic step taken by one of Basil Seal's cronies, a baronet, in *Put Out More Flags*. No wonder Basil concludes that the war is becoming like a club enclosure on a racecourse – 'If you aren't wearing the right badge they won't let you in.'

Evelyn had other worries. Laura was pregnant again, and he had to find a tenant for Piers Court, which was too big and costly to maintain in wartime. Luckily some Dominican teaching nuns, in search of premises for their school, agreed to take the house for a rent of £600 a year. The Waughs moved south-west to Pixton Park, the Herbert family's large house in Somerset. Noisy, crowded, disorderly and dog-ridden at the best of times – it was the model for 'Boot Magna Hall' in *Scoop* – Pixton was now even less appealing to Evelyn because it was overrun with evacuee children. Within a few days he had retreated to his old bolt-hole at Chagford. There, in limbo, he got to grips with *Work Suspended*, his 'spiffing' new novel.

Evelyn thought he had never written better. He was employing a new technique – the first-person narrative – and a new tone of voice, measured and reflective. John Plant, the narrator, is a smug, solipsistic writer of polished whodunits whose methodical way of life is shattered by the death of his father, a conventional portrait painter with a profitable line in forgery and a contrary temperament, who is knocked down while crossing the road. Plant gets writer's block, falls unrequitedly in love with the pregnant wife of a friend and is harried by the driver of the car that killed his father, a seedy, temporary-gentleman type called Atwater whose habitat is the arterial road. The novel was dedicated to the American man of letters Alexander Woolcott, who had pronounced Evelyn 'the nearest thing to a genius' among the young English writers of his time.

Then in late November, shortly after the birth of his first son, Auberon ('Bron'), Evelyn's networking paid off. Thanks to the intervention of Winston Churchill's Private Parliamentary Secretary, Brendan Bracken, at the Admiralty, he learnt that he was now a candidate for a commission in the Royal Marines. The marines were expanding so rapidly that they were handing out commissions on the spot, rather than requiring candidates to attend an Officers' Training Unit first – an experience Evelyn would probably not have relished. As it was he failed his medical, but was accepted at the interview which followed. That evening he drank rum on top of several bottles of champagne and was sick early the following morning, an appropriate beginning to a military career that was clouded by hangovers. On 7 December he reported for duty at the marines' barracks in Chatham.

Waugh's War
1940–5

Brain in an army is like a nail in one's shoe, out of place
if it is too sharp or hasn't been turned down.

Major-General 'Chink' Dorman-Smith

If, as Ann Fleming alleged, Evelyn liked things to go wrong, then
his military career must have afforded him much satisfaction. Of
the three operations in which he took part the first, Dakar, was
a fiasco; the second, Bardia, a farcical shambles; and the third,
Crete, an ignominious defeat. No blame attached to Evelyn for
any of these; indeed his conduct under fire on Crete was exemplary. But his subsequent failure to find a place for himself in the
battle was nobody's fault but his own. Everywhere he went he
was regarded as troublesome and offensive. Commanding
officers passed him on like a live grenade. In February 1940 he
had announced, 'I am proud to say that I have ceased to be a
writer and am now a Second-Lieutenant in the Royal Marines.'
Five years later, on the day before VE day, he wrote in his diary:
'It is pleasant to end the war in plain clothes, writing. I remember at the start of it all writing to Frank Pakenham that its value
for us would be to show us finally that we are not "men of
action". I took longer than him to learn it.'

Evelyn's problem with authority was that while he held
very conservative views he was, at bottom, an anarchist, who
could not conceal the disdain he felt for most of his superiors.

Abnegation, which all soldiers must learn to practise, was anathema to him. The notion that you saluted the uniform, not the man, passed him by. In *Officers and Gentlemen* there is a revealing passage involving the hero, Guy Crouchback, and his commanding officer, Tommy Backhouse:

> In all his military service Guy never ceased to marvel at the effortless transitions of intercourse between equality and superiority. It was a figure no temporary officer ever learned to cut... At Bellamy's he and Tommy were amiable acquaintances, as they had been years before. Last night they had been close friends. Today they were Colonel and Subaltern.

Guy, an unassertive fellow, does not repine. But all too often Evelyn took offence, behaving in an insolent and insubordinate manner that eventually made him 'so unpopular as to be unemployable'. A classic instance occurred when a general rebuked him for drinking too much in the mess before dinner. 'You can't expect me to change the habits of a lifetime for a whim of yours,' retorted Evelyn. He belonged in the awkward squad. Malcolm Muggeridge, noting how uncomfortable he looked in uniform, compared him to 'a parcel that had been delivered to the wrong address'. Pansy Pakenham's sister Mary made a similar point. He was, she thought, 'one of the few people who was not made more distinguished-looking by being in uniform'. And yet there was a part of him that desperately wanted to conform. He told Tom Burns that becoming a Catholic was like 'joining a regiment with traditions and rules which he never questioned', and to begin with, like Guy Crouchback and the Halberdiers, he did his utmost to act the part of an officer in the marines, even growing a moustache, an embellishment he sported intermittently for the rest of his life.

Evelyn's view of warfare was as sanguinary as that of the bellicose Brigadier Ben Ritchie-Hook in *Men at Arms*. He did not see how victory was possible without 'wholesale slaughter'. Once it became apparent that instead of 'biffing the enemy' the marines, like most of the Army after Dunkirk, would be restricted to home defence, he began to fret. The prospect of sharing a mess indefinitely with people who didn't understand his jokes added to his impatience. His brother officers, who steered clear of him off duty, were recruited from the same sort of humdrum young men with whom Alec had once played rugger (in *Men at Arms* Lieutenant Leonard plays scrum-half for Alec's old club, Rosslyn Park), a far cry from the guardees and landowners he met in Buck's, the smart, slightly raffish club he had joined in succession to the Savile. Hearing that volunteers were needed for a new independent raiding force he again applied to Brendan Bracken, now established in 10 Downing Street as Churchill's *consigliere*. But before anything could be settled he found himself aboard a troopship bound for the French West African port of Dakar, in an expedition to install a Free French force there in place of the Vichy garrison.

In the event, as Evelyn told Laura, bloodshed was avoided at the cost of honour. They all returned home with their tails between their legs. But thanks to Bracken there was good news awaiting him: he was being seconded to Number 8 Commando, under the command of an old acquaintance, the dashing Colonel Bob Laycock. It would mean reverting from acting-captain to lieutenant, but as he also told Laura, the prestige of becoming a commando more than outweighed any loss of rank. The Commandos were at the sharp end of a new body called Combined Operations, designed to take the fight to the enemy by means of hit-and and-run amphibious raids. At that time they were stationed at Largs, a seaside resort about twenty miles from Glasgow, where the richer officers went to dine every evening. No. 8 Commando was feudal in character: its officers belonged in the stud book and were recruited from clubs like Buck's and White's. They were anticipating a long war and wanted to spend it among friends.

Evelyn's joy at soldiering with these uninhibited aristos – 'nothing could be less like the marines' – was tempered by his relative poverty. They had large private incomes; he had large debts. Even with allowances a lieutenant's pay did not go far, particularly since he was remitting £15 a month to Laura. She was experiencing a difficult third pregnancy, and on 1 December 1940 gave birth to a daughter, Mary, who died shortly afterwards. Arthur, never reconciled to Evelyn's *perversion* to Rome', blamed the priests and their opposition to birth control. He may have been right. Evelyn's epitaph on Mary – 'Poor little girl, she was not wanted' – reveals his ambivalence towards a pregnancy that he admitted was 'regretted by all'. Before the war was over Laura gave birth to two more daughters, Margaret ('Meg') and Harriet ('Hatty'); another son, James, was born in 1946, followed by Septimus in 1950. Later, with a nod to Lord Chesterfield, Evelyn would write: 'Of children as of procreation: the pleasure is momentary, the posture ridiculous, the expense damnable.' If her grandson Alex is correct, Laura was equally disenchanted, particularly with her daughters. During the war she preferred the role of camp follower to mother, leaving her children at Pixton Park whenever Evelyn asked her to join him at his latest posting. 'My mother did not feature in any particular way throughout those six years of my life at Pixton,' recalled Bron.

Relieved as he was to be shot of the marines, Evelyn retained enough of their ethos to note how indolent by comparison the officers of 8 Commando were: 'Nobody even pretended to work outside working hours.' He thought, however, that their 'gaiety and independence' would prove invaluable in action, the promise of which arrived with their posting to North Africa, where after a five-week voyage round the Cape of Good Hope they arrived in March 1941. Evelyn had hoped to become a troop commander; instead, after intervals as a liaison officer and adjutant, he was made intelligence officer, in which capacity he took part in the futile raid on Bardia.

This was the sort of 'butcher and bolt' night operation for which the Commandos were intended. Bardia, on the Libyan coast, was a big transport depot defended by a coastal battery and a garrison of 2,000 Italian troops. Or so it was believed. In fact the Italians had abandoned the town and spiked the guns. Determined to do some damage the raiders set fire to a tyre dump, thus alerting the enemy to their presence. In the hasty evacuation sixty men went to the wrong beach and were later captured. The ramp of Evelyn's landing craft jammed and was only raised in the nick of time. The one casualty on either side was a British officer mistakenly shot by friendly fire. In the authorized account he subsequently wrote Evelyn claimed the raid was a success because the enemy, mindful of Bardia's vulnerability, reinforced it with a large detachment of tanks and armoured cars from their front line which they could ill afford to lose. But no further action was required of the Commandos, now designated 'Layforce', who remained under canvas in the desert. Like everyone else Evelyn chafed at their inactivity. Was it to brood like Achilles in his tent that they had come all this way?

Events then took a hand. On 20 May, having occupied Greece, the Germans launched an airborne attack on Crete, which was defended by several thousand heterogeneous British, Dominion and Greek troops. The Germans had command of the air and once they captured the largest airfield their ultimate victory was assured. For the British what now mattered was evacuating as many men as possible from Sphakia, a tiny port in the south. On 26 May Layforce landed on the island to provide a rearguard, Evelyn accompanying Colonel Laycock as his intelligence officer. He gave two accounts of his experiences, one factual, one fictional. In both cases the shame he felt at participating in such a debacle was very evident. It marked the beginning of his disillusionment with the Allied cause that is so apparent from his diaries and provides the motif for *Sword of Honour*. Like Scott-King, the eponymous hero of his novella *Scott-King's Modern*

Europe, he came to see the war – in which he never rose above the rank of captain – as 'a sweaty tug of war between two teams of indistinguishable louts'.

For much of his time on Crete Evelyn was employed by Laycock as his scout, a dangerous job but one which put him fully 'in the picture', which would not have been the case had he been a troop commander, whose horizon was necessarily limited. It was not a pretty sight. Most of the troops he saw were at the end of their tether, intent only on saving their skins. Officers were as demoralized as their men, one in particular witnessed by Evelyn, the model for his character Major 'Fido' Hound, cracking up completely, though as a member of Layforce he was only exposed to bombing and strafing for a few days. Evelyn himself did not fire a shot in anger; he claimed that his most valuable piece of equipment in action was a pillow. His bravery was defined by his refusal to take cover when Stukas appeared, which did not endear him to troops in the vicinity, who had no wish to draw attention to themselves.

Layforce were ordered to hold the line around Sphakia for as long as they could, only embarking when all other 'fighting troops' had been taken off. This was a recipe for capture which the ambitious Colonel Laycock did not intend to follow. He persuaded the senior British officer left on the island that he and his headquarters, including Evelyn, were fighting troops who took precedence over the 'rabble' on the beach. As the last ships were preparing to leave he led his men to the shore, commandeered a motor boat and then clambered aboard a destroyer, leaving 'Major Hound' and the rest of Layforce behind. Equally unwilling to be captured, Evelyn connived at Laycock's casuistry about fighting troops. But it has since been urged that his shame at what he saw on Crete was compounded by guilt. Contemptuous of those who cried '*Sauve qui peut*', he submitted to that impera-tive himself and 'did a bunk', albeit at the behest of his com-manding officer. Loyal to Laycock, who became a major-general, Evelyn never breathed a word against him over Crete. In *Officers and Gentlemen*, dedicated to Laycock, his doppelganger, Colonel Tommy Backhouse, conveniently breaks his leg en route to Crete, thus absolving Evelyn from the need to examine his conduct.

In Egypt what remained of Layforce was disbanded and Evelyn resumed life as a marine. Never one to dissemble he made plain his disgust at our poor showing in Crete, defeatist talk that can't have advanced his cause as a soldier. Nor can his mood have been improved by the news that Russia was now an ally. In July he began a long voyage home that took him as far afield as Trinidad and Iceland. On arrival he was pleased to learn that in his absence he had been elected a member of White's, for 200 years the haunt of grandees. But as an elderly lieutenant of marines he was largely surplus to military requirements and spent the next nine months being 'buggered about', his hopes of commanding a company unfulfilled. At one point he was examined by an Army psychiatrist, who was nonplussed by Evelyn's Parthian shot: 'Why have you asked me nothing about the most important thing in a man's life, his religion?'

But Evelyn's mind was not always on higher things. In November 1942, a few weeks after the birth of his daughter Meg, he and another commando, Lord Jellicoe, were involved in a brawl over some girls at a dive in Wardour Street. Evelyn suffered a black eye and the embarrassment of seeing the fracas, and their appearance next day at Bow Street Magistrate's Court, reported in the *Evening Standard*. Perhaps the nightclub scene and its aftermath in *Brideshead Revisited* owes something to this incident.

Eventually Bob Laycock, whose star was in the ascendant, rode to Evelyn's rescue. He wanted him for the new Commando Brigade he was forming, and when the marines refused to release him, arranged for him to be seconded to his own regiment, The Blues. So Evelyn had achieved a notable civil and military double: membership of White's and a commission in the Horse Guards. When Anthony Powell, a wry observer of Evelyn's social progress, heard of this, he commented: 'One cannot but admire such pertinacity of purpose.' But as someone who said he never worked harder than during the war, much of which he spent in the unglamorous role of a military liaison officer, Powell would not have admired the sottish life Evelyn began to lead when, as before, he was attached to Laycock's headquarters. 'I think we are the only mess in Europe that consistently drinks claret, port and brandy at dinner,' boasted Evelyn, whose diary at this time invites the canting call to order, 'Don't you know there's a war on?'

A modern reader, accustomed to think of special forces like the Commandos as 'lean, mean, fighting machines', might justifiably wonder why Laycock was so keen to have him. One explanation is that Laycock, an educated soldier, relished the pith that Evelyn brought to human intercourse. Another is that he could draft. On one occasion he boiled down twenty-five pages on the future of Commandos to a single sheet. Later, when Colonel Bill Stirling, the founder of the SAS, wanted to pitch for its expansion, it was to Evelyn he turned for a brief. But work of this kind was all too rare. He was often bored, and this made him bloody-minded. And when he was bloody-minded the wit that could entrance turned corrosive; people became tongue-tied in his presence, inviting further snubs. Laycock's patience wore thin. He warned Evelyn that he was becoming 'so unpopular as to be unemployable'.

(Evelyn remained a loose cannon, as witness this anecdote from the former Governor-General of Australia, Lord de Lisle. A Grenadier Guardsman VC, like his father-in-law, Lord Gort, Lord de Lisle found himself alone in the dining room at Pratt's club with someone he described as 'a little old man with an ear trumpet' who drunkenly proclaimed that the tradition of the Foot Guards was one of cowardice. What prompted Evelyn to deliver this slur is unknown. Lord de Lisle's response was to say 'Fuck off' and leave the room.)

Evelyn abandoned *Work Suspended* because he thought the people about whom, and for whom, it was written were on the way out. But to amuse himself on the long voyage back from Egypt he began a new novel, set during the Phoney War, about the same sort of people as those he'd written off. Although he considered it a minor work, *Put Out More Flags* (1942) contains some of the funniest passages Evelyn ever wrote, notably the abortive interview Basil Seal has with a Guards' colonel. As well as Basil, who reappears as a Lord of Misrule, it features a character based on another of Evelyn's equivocal Oxford contemporaries, Brian Howard, whom he had already invoked as 'Johnnie Hoop' in *Vile Bodies*. The most brazen of the Bright Young People, a man of style but little substance, Howard, like Connolly, went left in the Thirties, much of which he spent vainly trying to keep his German boyfriend from being conscripted by the Nazis. In the novel he's called Ambrose Silk, a precious man of letters who has attempted, with some success, to mimic the dour proletarian art of the Thirties. But in his heart he knows it's all rot, which proves that he, like Basil, has Evelyn's sympathy, which does not extend to Parsnip and Pimpernel – for which read Auden and Isherwood – the two left-wing scribes whose flight to America so agitates their friends.

Evelyn had no qualms about libelling Peter Rodd again. He insisted that however recognizable a character was no offence would be taken by the libellee provided you said he was attractive to women – which was certainly the case with Prod. This made life hard for Mrs Rodd, Nancy Mitford, and soon after the war began they separated.[7] Evelyn was very fond of Nancy, who in early days had given him several tips about upper-class life. In return he helped her with her novels, particularly the two that made her name after the war, *The Pursuit of Love* and *Love in a Cold Climate*. During the war she worked at Heywood Hill in Curzon Street, more of a club than a bookshop, and it was there that Evelyn, flown with wine, would go to buy books and hear the latest gossip, most of it emanating from the milieu depicted here by the astute Canadian diplomat and diarist, Charles Ritchie:

In love as in conversation a flavour of insolence is appreciated. With both sexes the thing admired is to do what you want just as long as you want and not a moment longer. Hence the speed at which people change partners in this game, which requires a good eye, a cool nerve and a capacity to take punishment as in any other kind of sport. Toughness is the favourite virtue. Any form of cry-babyishness… is taboo except among pansies, in whom it is recognized as an innate characteristic which does not affect their essential toughness… Their gossip is so frank, so abundant and so detailed it is a wonder their lives are not even more complicated than they are. Discretion is looked upon as a paltry virtue like thrift. Their closest friends' reputations are ripped to pieces at the tops of their voices usually in a restaurant. Among themselves they practice a mixture of delicate sympathy and charming attention, alternated with dive-bombing attacks of brutal frankness. Rows are frequent but seldom lasting. They stick by each other in misfortune with the loyalty the English usually show to their friends.

Ritchie placed Evelyn at the heart of this set. But a reminder of how far he had travelled to arrive there occurred on 26 June 1943, when Arthur died. Evelyn had seen little of him since the war began, but because Alec, who was lucky not to be taken prisoner again when France fell, was serving in Syria, he had to arrange the funeral and see to it that Catherine, their mother, was properly provided for. Twenty years later, when he had had plenty of opportunity to reflect on the bitter joys of parenthood, Evelyn saw his father in a benign light, praising him for creating a warm and stable home. And Anthony Powell, who observed them both together in the Twenties when Evelyn was at his most feckless, thought they got on perfectly well. But Arthur knew he set his son's teeth on edge, and there can be no question that Evelyn never forgave him for favouring Alec, a preference Arthur extended to their respective wives: Joan delighted him, whereas he couldn't fathom Laura at all.

There is a macabre footnote to the story of father and son. In *A Little Learning* Evelyn says Arthur was physically brave, citing his decision to have several of his teeth removed without anaesthetic. Just turned sixty Evelyn followed suit; Bron was convinced this hastened his demise. (Bizarrely, an equally harrowing visit to the dentist did for Aubrey Herbert, Laura's father.)

Arthur died at an inopportune moment for Evelyn, who was granted compassionate leave just when preparations were in hand for the invasion of Sicily. With Laycock already in North Africa, Evelyn's enemies, who included Laycock's much decorated second-in-command, the highland chieftain Lord Lovat, took steps to ensure that he remained behind. Evelyn returned Lovat's dislike with interest, referring to him in his diary as 'Mickey Rooney' and caricaturing him as the appalling Trimmer in *Sword of Honour*. But in 1943 Lovat held all the aces. He ordered Evelyn to spend at least six weeks getting fit at the unit's base in Scotland, correctly surmising that he would protest at this. In fact Evelyn protested to a higher authority, unaware that this officer shared Lord Lovat's low opinion of him, which was conveyed in no uncertain terms. So Evelyn had no option but to resign from the Special Services Brigade (as Laycock's Commando was now styled) and return to the Royal Horse Guards, whose barracks at Windsor was full of 'middle-aged, embittered subalterns' like him. Soon afterwards he met another officer left behind by Laycock, 'exuberant' at getting his move order after some deft schmoozing. 'I think England is the only country where people resort to bribery to get *into* the war,' he wrote.

To give his life some purpose Evelyn decided to try and save the soul of his old friend Hubert Duggan, a lapsed Catholic who had gone into a decline following the sudden death of his beloved mistress a few months before. The stepson of Lord Curzon, who had married his wealthy American mother after her first husband, an Irishman, had died of drink in Argentina, Duggan, never very healthy, was now at death's door. He seemed to want to return to the church, but only if he were not required to repent of his life with his mistress. Against the wishes of Duggan's mother and sister Evelyn brought a priest to his bedside and was rewarded by the sight of Duggan crossing himself after receiving the last rites. This proof of God's grace had momentous consequences, as he later explained to Monsignor Ronald Knox:

I am glad you became reconciled to [*Brideshead*] in the end. It was, of course, all about the death bed. I was present at almost exactly that scene... when a friend of mine, whom we thought in his final coma and stubbornly impenitent, whose womenfolk would only let the priest in because they thought him unconscious, did exactly that, making the sign of the cross. It was profoundly affecting and I wrote the book about that scene.

Oddly enough Evelyn seems to have been unaware that Duggan, who was in the same house at Eton as Anthony Powell, became the model for Powell's character Stringham as a schoolboy, in *A Dance to the Music of Time*. Stringham turns to drink, like Duggan's elder brother Alfred, who with Evelyn's encouragement sobered up after the war and wrote several historical novels.

Shortly after Hubert Duggan died Evelyn had his fortieth birthday. Amazingly he was selected to join the embryonic Special Air Service, and in January 1944 attended a parachute course. His first drop was exhilarating, but then he landed awkwardly and broke his leg. So ended his hopes of martial preferment. Downcast at the prospect of stagnating at Windsor he took the bold step of requesting three months' leave without pay to write a novel, shrewdly sending a copy of his request to Brendan Bracken, by now the Minister of Information. Although Bracken did not reply it seems likely that he supported the request, and for a month Evelyn was in Mrs Cobb's care at Chagford, completing over 30,000 words of his new 'magnum opus', *Brideshead Revisited*. Then he got a nasty shock: the War Office had cancelled his leave. So began a protracted struggle, in which Evelyn marshaled all the forces at his disposal to frustrate the War Office's efforts to employ him. They did not give up easily, and every two or three weeks he had to leave Chagford and go to London to demonstrate how unfitted he was for whatever they had in mind. Finally, thanks to the combined efforts of Laycock and Bill Stirling, he was granted enough leave to finish the book, which he did on 8 June, less than six months after he began it.

His leave over, Evelyn reported for duty at the SAS base in Perthshire, where Stirling's successor as commanding officer, Bryan Franks, though personally fond of Evelyn, was determined to keep him away from the troops. Appropriately it was thanks to an equally recalcitrant cog in the military machine, Winston Churchill's son Randolph, that Evelyn was at last accommodated. As an earnest of his support for Tito's partisans in Yugoslavia the Prime Minister had consented to Randolph's joining the British military mission there. Unimpressed by the social credentials of his brother officers, Randolph, to whom Evelyn had dedicated *Put Out More Flags*, soon insisted that Evelyn join him, on the plausible grounds that Croatia, their next destination, was a Catholic province. He assumed, wrongly, that he and Evelyn, fellow members of White's, would be boon companions. But as Evelyn ruefully acknowledged after several disputatious weeks together, 'no one else would have chosen me, nor would anyone else have accepted him'.

Disliked by his mother, indulged by his father, whose shadow he could never escape, Randolph Churchill was a classic case of someone who wanted the palm without the dust and never got over its being withheld. He had Basil Seal's effrontery and, when young and handsome, some of his appeal, which may be why Evelyn was drawn to him. But as the bloom went off him, so did his disaffection grow. Opinionated and obstreperous, his tantrums were legendary. 'Mummy, what is that man *for*?' a child is supposed to have asked after seeing him lose his rag. By 1944 he had become one of the most unpopular men in the British Army, rumoured, as was the case with Evelyn, to be more in danger from his own men than the enemy. The removal from circulation at once of these two hard cases must have gratified their superiors, whose reaction to the news that their plane had crashed in Croatia can only be guessed at. Both were lucky to survive, though their injuries were such that they had to be flown back to the Italian port of Bari for treatment.

Before this an incident occurred when Evelyn, for once, was at a loss for words. Contemptuous of Tito, whom he saw as a puppet of the hated Stalin, Evelyn affected to believe that he was really a woman because he didn't appear to shave. Word of this slander must have reached Tito, whose headquarters were then on the Dalmatian island of Vis. Emerging from the sea after a bathe, his masculinity clearly apparent, Tito was confronted by Evelyn and Randolph, to whom he was introduced by Brigadier Fitzroy Maclean, the head of the British mission. 'Ask Captain Waugh,' said Tito to Maclean, 'why he thinks I am a woman.' This Maclean did, and answer came there none. (There is an amusing footnote to this story. In 1953 when Tito, now estranged from Stalin, was in London on an official visit, *Punch* caused a stir when it ran a cartoon of him as a coy Restoration beauty being wooed by a rakish Churchill.)

The partisans' attitude towards the Allies had always been, at best, grudging. By September 1944, when Evelyn and Randolph returned to Croatia, relations had deteriorated because it was clear that with the Allies bogged down in Italy, only the Red Army could liberate Yugoslavia. But since the Germans were still dangerous and the Partisans relied on the Allies for arms, equipment and medical supplies, they could not afford to be too hostile. Billeted in a farmhouse near the Croatian spa of Topusko, Evelyn and Randolph had little to occupy them and soon began to quarrel. Evelyn's mood was not improved by the absence of his two staples, wine and cigars. Unlike Randolph, who was frequently drunk, he refused to touch the local hooch, *rakija*, a purgative plum brandy. His sobriety provoked Randolph, though probably not as much as his description of Winston Churchill as a writer of 'sham Augustan prose'. When Lord Birkenhead joined them a month later he was immediately reminded of 'a pair of belligerent robins'.

The son of the Prime Minister's old crony F.E. Smith, Birkenhead soaked up some of Randolph's blather, but contributed more of his own. 'Of conversation as I love it,' wrote Evelyn, '– a fantasy growing in the telling, apt repartee, argument based on accepted postulates, spontaneous reminiscences and quotation – they know nothing. All their noise and laughter is in the retelling of memorable sayings of their respective fathers or other public figures; even with this vast repertoire they repeat themselves every day or two – sometimes within an hour.' To try and silence Randolph the others bet him £10 each that he couldn't read the Bible right through in a fortnight. Far from silencing him, the Bible generated a fresh torrent of blather, including the mantra, 'God, isn't God a shit!' Not surprisingly, he lost the bet.

In December they left Topusko and Evelyn was reassigned to Dubrovnik, having obtained permission from Maclean to report on the religious situation there. He was able to prove that Tito and his followers were persecuting Catholics, but made himself very unpopular by drawing attention to the fact. In the Balkans all that now mattered to the British was Greece, where their interests were threatened by a communist insurgency. They had no comparable stake in Yugoslavia, and were reconciled to its being taken over by Tito, who had, it was felt, a genuine case against the Catholic Church because of its association with the *Ustaše*, the murderous fascist militia that had terrorized the country following the German invasion. Evelyn's report, 'Church and State in Liberated Croatia', was suppressed by the Foreign Office and his efforts to publicise his findings got no further than two letters to *The Times*. By then the war in Europe was over and the world about to turn upside down, putting the Common Man on top. In the twenty-one years that remained to him Evelyn never altered his perspective to allow for this social revolution. Like Charles Ryder and Sebastian in *Brideshead Revisited*, he was *contra mundum*.

Luxury not Lionisation
1945–52

> But this is terrible – *they've* elected a Labour Government,
> and *the country* will never stand for that!
>
> *Overheard at the Savoy Hotel, 26 July 1945*

Some of Evelyn's most productive hours in Yugoslavia were spent correcting the proofs of *Brideshead Revisited*, for which he had the highest hopes. In terms of sales these were to be realized: the book became an international bestseller, casting Evelyn in the 'disquieting' role of celebrity. But as always he was eager for the approval of his friends, and this was not as wholehearted as he would have wished. On the dust jacket he had warned that the book 'was *not* meant to be funny', but even before publication he learnt that Cyril Connolly's latest party piece was his droll imitation of Lord Marchmain reciting his titles on his deathbed. Nancy Mitford was encouraging, but regretted that Ryder, the narrator, lacked sparkle. He's meant to lack sparkle, said Evelyn; the book's not about him. Then what do the Flytes all see in him? asked Nancy.

Ryder's lack of sparkle contrasts with such gaudy figures as Anthony Blanche and Rex Mottram, both brilliantly brought to life on television. Blanche has some of the best lines in the book, though this may not have consoled the two people he resembled, Evelyn's old friend Harold Acton, and Acton's schoolmate, Brian Howard. Mottram, the crass, colonial go-getter is a caricature of Brendan Bracken, whose efforts on Evelyn's behalf evidently counted for nothing. Yet Mottram has an impudent gusto that recalls Basil Seal and makes Ryder seem supercilious as well as dim. It may offend some people to say it, but his matter of fact dealings with Father Mowbray don't sound so very different from those Evelyn had with the priest who instructed him, Father Martin D'Arcy. Another easily identifiable character is Maurice Bowra, alias Mr Samgrass, the unctuous young don hired as Sebastian's minder by Lady Marchmain. But instead of complaining, Bowra confounded Evelyn by saying that Samgrass was 'the best thing in the whole book'. He and Evelyn could be very disparaging behind each others' backs, but never face to face – probably because both realized that they were so well matched that any victory would be pyrrhic.

Unlike modern critics, Evelyn's friends were not unduly bothered by *Brideshead*'s snobbery. Most of them were snobbish themselves, though not necessarily about the same things as Evelyn. An exception was Lady Pansy Lamb, the former Pansy Pakenham, who thought there was little to choose between the sort of people she met at 1920s deb dances (to which Evelyn was not invited) and Hooper, the plebeian young officer who exemplifies the debased post-war world that Ryder dreads. 'Most of the girls were drab and dowdy and the men even more so,' she told Evelyn. They were 'respectable, well-to-do, narrow minded with ideals no way differing from Hooper's except that their basic ration was larger. Hooperism is only the transcription in cheaper terms of the upper class outlook of 1920 and like most mass-reproductions is not flattering to its originators.'

Evelyn got a vote of confidence from the catholics he knew, though one or two blushed at the sex. But for those of his friends who weren't catholics – the majority – the religion was an issue. They had never felt 'a twitch upon the thread' and were unconvinced by it. But even a staunch protestant like Henry Yorke, who was 'shocked and hurt' when Lord Marchmain crossed himself, acknowledged the beauty of the elegiac Oxford episodes and the skill with which Evelyn depicted Brideshead

Castle itself (one critic thought the hero of the book was not a person, but a building). Like Ryder, an architectural painter, Evelyn was passionate about architecture, particularly Augustan architecture. This had a bearing on the story. Because of the restrictions under which they then lived no recusant family, however distinguished, could have built a baroque pile like Brideshead. Consequently Lord Marchmain had to be a convert, something that is often overlooked.

Evelyn later excused the 'wedding cake' prose to which fastidious readers like Maurice Bowra objected on the grounds that it was a reaction against wartime privations. In fact, as his diaries show, he lacked for very little; the only time he went without was in Yugoslavia, by which time he had written *Brideshead*. An alternative explanation is that at long last he had surrendered to his Muse, and as an act of contrition piled it on rather thick. Style was what mattered to him now. 'I regard writing not as investigation of character but as an exercise in the use of language,' he told an interviewer, 'and with this I am obsessed.' Second only to his religion Evelyn revered the 'might and scope' of the English language. Woe betide those, like Stephen Spender, who misused it: 'To see Spender fumbling with our rich and delicate language is to experience all the horror of seeing a Sèvres vase in the hands of a chimpanzee.' He was equally aghast at clumsy speech, which had not made for ease in the mess.

For most of his adult life Evelyn had been in debt, sometimes heavily. Now, as an age of austerity dawned, he was 'stinking rich', able to spend £100 a week on trifles at a time when the cost of a three-course meal was not supposed to exceed five shillings. Even before the spoils of *Brideshead* became available he had plenty to spare. *Put Out More Flags* had outsold all his other novels, and for most of the war MGM paid him a retainer of £10 a week in the vain hope that he would write for them when out of uniform. But Labour's sensational victory in the 1945 election, with its promise of 'Fair Shares for All', threatened the vision he had of himself as a gentleman living his own life. Convinced that England was done for he seriously considered moving to Ireland to escape the 'Attlee terror', and meanwhile asked Peters to ensure that his earnings did not exceed £5,000 a year, thus limiting his tax bill. Peters was able to do this because since 1938 he had acted as Evelyn's banker, as well as his agent, doling out money as and when it was needed, but always with an eye on his client's tax bill.

Evelyn knew he was unlikely to hit the jackpot twice, so his reluctance to see most of it go in tax was understandable.[8] But he was lucky to have such an astute collaborator as Peters, whose importance cannot be exaggerated. Without Peters Evelyn would certainly have been in the poorhouse, possibly even in prison. Aware that American contracts gave more scope for 'legal hanky-panky', i.e. exploitation, Peters ensured that a substantial part of Evelyn's American earnings could legitimately be classed as 'expenses', making them tax-free. Endlessly patient and resourceful, he not only obtained the best of terms for his very demanding client, he also devised all manner of tax-evasion schemes, the most creative of which – the 'Save the Children Fund' – was eventually undone by the Inland Revenue, but not before Evelyn had derived great benefit from it. Another way Evelyn could thwart the tax-gatherers was to make over some of his foreign royalties to catholic charities, as he had done ten years before with all the royalties from *Campion*. He must have given away tens of thousands of pounds like this and, if his motives were not entirely unselfish, the ends appeared to justify the means.

Paying lots of tax was one penalty of writing a bestseller. Another was fan mail, much of it from American women who assumed, wrongly, that his 'friendship and confidence' were included in the price of a book. Evelyn despised familiarity. It was another of the reasons why he was such an uncongenial messmate. 'Intimacy, Formality and Servility' were the only human relationships he could abide. But while quite prepared (as we have seen) to snub a fan in person, even Evelyn drew the line at delivering a collective snub. Instead, for a large fee from *Life* magazine, he wrote 'Fan-Fare', a chatty piece in which he vouchsafed a few personal details, answered some of the most common questions put by readers of *Brideshead* and indicated what to expect from him in future: a preoccupation with style, and man in his relation to God.

But God was absent from Evelyn's next offering, *Scott-King's Modern Europe*, which sounds like a school textbook but is in fact a short cautionary tale about the misadventures of a misanthropic middle-aged English Classics master who's invited to the tercentenary celebrations of Bellorius, the obscure Renaissance poet whose Latin epic he has spent years translating into Spenserian stanzas. Neutralia, Scott-King's destination, is partly based on Franco's Spain, where in 1946 Evelyn and his friend Douglas Woodruff attended just such a celebration, for an equally obscure seventeenth-century jurist. Expecting a jolly two weeks in the sun (it was a wet summer at home) with a bit of sightseeing thrown in, they found themselves far below the salt with regard to transport and accommodation, and bored to tears by the proceedings. Evelyn was not impressed and never returned. As for Scott-King, who has a far worse time of it than Evelyn, he learns on the last page that fifteen fewer boys will now be specializing in Classics. Nearly seventy years later the headmaster's take on this sounds oddly familiar: 'Parents are not interested in producing the "complete man" any more. They want to qualify their boys for jobs in the modern world. You can hardly blame them, can you?'

But Scott-King can and does. 'I think it would be very wicked indeed to do anything to fit a boy for the modern world,' he replies, precisely the sort of diehard remark that Evelyn himself would become notorious for uttering.

Appalled though he was by living in 'Welfaria' under the Labour Government Evelyn eventually decided it would not do for him to move to Ireland; he must stay and face the music. No one was more relieved at this than Laura Waugh. West Country born and bred she had no desire to live in a gloomy pile among strangers, separated from her children's schools by the Irish Sea. We learn this from Evelyn's letters and diaries, not from Laura herself. An enigmatic figure even to her children, her side of the story – what it was to be Mrs Evelyn Waugh – remains unwritten. We know she was painfully shy and a poor correspondent, that she had several difficult pregnancies, that she played no part in Evelyn's London life and that she appeared happiest tending the small herd of milking cows she kept in the paddocks beside Piers Court. The rest is conjecture. Evelyn was a very needy man. He wanted her with him at all times except when he was working, or letting off steam in London. But that was not the whole story. At Piers Court he presided over a large and 'ceremonious' household, the running of which he delegated to her. This was a tall order for someone with no domestic training. In their early years the children – 'Your children', Evelyn called them – were also her responsibility. Evelyn never had to cope with the pram in the hall and boasted of his Olympian manner towards its occupants. 'I have numerous children whom I see once a day for ten, I hope, awe-inspiring minutes,' he told the readers of *Life*.

But Laura was no squaw. Francis Donaldson, the Waughs' perceptive neighbour, said she 'could not trim her personality to suit his whims'. It took Evelyn a while to realize this. Utterly unlike the worldly women he saw in London in most other respects, she shared with them the self-assurance bestowed by generations of privilege. Evelyn resented this when it operated against him and it probably accounts for his antagonism towards Laura's lumpish brother Auberon, whom he considered a waste of space. He and Mary Herbert were reconciled following the success of *Brideshead*. But it was a great sorrow to Laura that Evelyn never got on with Auberon and would visit Pixton only on sufferance.

Though Evelyn often gave the impression of thinking of no one but himself he must have grasped that Laura had a far harder time of it during the war than he did. Like most of the population she needed a good holiday, and thanks to the interest shown in *Brideshead* by Hollywood, Evelyn was in a position to provide this. Explaining that 'luxury, not lionisation' was his requirement, he got Peters to arrange a five-star freebie to Hollywood and back, ostensibly to negotiate with the 'Californian savages', in reality to spend several weeks in clover at MGM's expense. But before they went Evelyn rather rashly decided to undergo a 'painful, costly and indelicate' operation for piles. He did this not because it was necessary – his symptoms were mild – but because unlike at home, he and Laura would be sharing a bedroom, and he wished to spare both of them the embarrassment that his anointing himself would occasion. His good deed did not go unpunished. The aftermath was agonizing and throughout the trip he needed a steady supply of painkillers.

As anticipated there was no meeting of minds between Evelyn and the moguls. They saw his novel as a love story, not as an example of God's grace in action. Evelyn wouldn't budge and the stand-off was resolved, ironically, when the Hays Office, responsible for enforcing the industry's strict moral code, rejected the script because it dealt sympathetically with divorce, a taboo subject. So to everyone's relief, the project was shelved. But the Waughs' time had not been wasted: Laura got the holiday she needed, replenished her wardrobe and was, for probably the first time in her married life, 'serenely happy'. For Evelyn, wearing his prospector's hat, southern California was a rich seam. He laughed up his sleeve at the stuffy English colony and their cricket club, the sort of place in which Alec, who never travelled without his MCC blazer, would have felt at home. But as he told Harold Acton, the revelation had been Forest Lawns cemetery, a Tivoli Gardens for the dead and the setting for 'a long short story' he was planning. Evelyn paid several visits to this sumptuous necropolis and even met the chief embalmer, famous for the 'personality smile' he gave each corpse, known as 'the loved one', the title Evelyn chose for his gruesomely funny 'novelette'.

Conscious of what he called the 'the Anglo-American impasse – never the twain shall meet', Evelyn wondered whether it would be wise to publish *The Loved One* in America at all. How would they react to Mr Joyboy's boast that 'there is something in the innocent appeal of a child that brings out a little more than the best in me'? But American skins were thicker than he supposed and like Jessica Mitford's 1963 exposé *The American Way of Death*, it was a bestseller on both sides of the pond, restoring his reputation as a satirist after the pomposity of *Brideshead*. As a favour to Cyril Connolly Evelyn offered *Horizon* first publication rights for the price of his subscription. The edition sold out, one copy finding its way to Moscow where a party hack, in a piece attacking *Horizon* and 'the gang of desperadoes' who wrote for it, decried 'The stench of corruption that rose from Waugh's nauseating book.'

Evelyn made three more trips to America, partly to thwart the tax-gatherers, partly because his hosts made it very worth his while, but also because he'd developed a keen interest in the American Catholic Church which was encouraged by his new friend, Clare Boothe Luce, a fervent catholic convert married to the owner of *Time* and *Life* magazines, Henry Luce. Thanks to Mrs Luce he was commissioned to write a long retrospective piece for *Life* on 'The American Epoch in the Catholic Church', the burden of which was that American catholics could teach their European brethren a thing or two. Much of his material was acquired during a lecture tour of catholic campuses, whose good work he applauded. He also praised the 'heroic fidelity of the Negro Catholics' in the face of insult and injury, an unusually enlightened view in the pre-civil rights era.

Evelyn's catholicism was now militant and inquisitorial. He believed wholeheartedly in hell and strove to convince his non-catholic friends, particularly devout Anglicans like John Betjeman, of the torments that awaited them should they persist in their folly. It is hard to imagine Graham Greene, Evelyn's only rival as an English catholic novelist, behaving like that. Indeed according to George Orwell, Greene saw hell as 'a sort of high-class night-club, entry to which was reserved for catholics only.' As with Evelyn and Cyril Connolly, there is a book to be written about him and Greene, comparing and contrasting their lives, their work and their beliefs. Not surprisingly Evelyn regarded Greene's catholicism as 'heretical'. He could never hope to agree with him, he said, 'this side of death'. And yet despite their many differences the two men had enormous respect for each other. When Evelyn died Greene said it was like losing your commanding officer. He was one of the few friends with whom Evelyn never fell out, a remarkable feat given Evelyn's intemperate nature and Greene's huge appetite for conflict.

No such harmony existed between Evelyn and Duff Cooper, an acquaintance rather than a friend, but one whom Evelyn saw a fair amount of by virtue of his being Diana Cooper's husband. Cooper had a short fuse that Evelyn could not resist lighting; but it was not just mischief that made him reach for a match. He blamed 'cad' Cooper, in his wartime role as Minister of Information, for two crimes: the vilification of P.G. Wodehouse for his wartime broadcasts from Germany, and the launch of the 'love-in' between Britain and the Soviet Union following the German invasion. Duff Cooper died before Evelyn broadcast his 'act of homage and reparation' to Wodehouse. But as early as 1942 Evelyn had begun to bait Cooper about the war, infuriating him by saying that he 'could see little difference between Hitler's new order and Virgil's idea of the Roman Empire'. Whether he seriously believed, as he later wrote in his diary, that with the Russians advancing on all fronts 'the Germans now represent Europe against the world', is debatable. But he thought Churchill deserved to lose in 1945 for deserting Poland, the country on whose behalf Britain went to war, and told Cooper to his face that Labour had won because Tories like him had emboldened the proles by cosying up to 'Uncle Joe' and lauding the USSR. Cooper's response was volcanic. 'It's rotten little rats like you who have brought about the downfall of the country,' he told Evelyn, accusing him of homosexuality, cowardice and pacifism, charges to which Evelyn made no answer. Cooper then showed that he too could tease by successfully proposing Evelyn's *bête noire*, the suave man of letters Peter Quennell, for White's.

Someone else who thought Wodehouse had had a raw deal was George Orwell, whom Evelyn visited in 1949 when Orwell, sinking fast, was in a sanatorium in Dursley, not far from Piers Court. Sadly, neither Evelyn nor Orwell, nor Evelyn's neighbour Frances Donaldson, who was also present, left a record of their meeting. All we have is this dry comment by Malcolm Muggeridge, who saw the funny side of both of them, and who together with Anthony Powell had set the meeting up: 'I should have loved to see them together, Waugh's country gentleman outfit and Orwell's proletarian one, both straight out of back numbers of *Punch*.'

Evelyn admired *Animal Farm* and *1984*, though in the letter he wrote to Orwell proposing his visit he took issue with the 'disappearance of the Church' in *1984*. He had made a similar point when reviewing a collection of Orwell's essays: 'Mr Orwell seems as unaware of the existence of his Christian neighbours as is, say, Sir Max Beerbohm of the urban proletariat.' Just before they met, Orwell had reviewed *Scott-King's Modern Europe* for the *New York Times*, finding it 'extremely readable', but marred by the 'diehard, know-nothing' Conservatism it appeared to endorse. As for Evelyn's religion, Orwell believed that 'One cannot really be Catholic and grown-up.' This assertion is contained in some notes he wrote for an unfinished essay on *Brideshead*. 'Waugh,' he concluded, 'is about as good a novelist as one can be (i.e. as novelists go today) while holding untenable opinions.' To Evelyn, of course, it was Orwell's humanism that was untenable. His next novel, *Helena*, which he had begun in 1946, was about a saint.

The mother of Constantine the Great, Saint Helena was beatified because she discovered what remained of the True Cross. Legend had it that she was a princess from Colchester, the departure point for Evelyn who imagined her as a striking flame-haired tomboy, very fond of horses and inclined, like Cordelia in *Brideshead*, to dismiss anything she doesn't understand as 'bosh'. She catches the eye of the future Emperor Constantius, a cold fish who whisks her off to Illyria, fathers Constantine, and then divorces her. But unlike her calculating son, who embraces Christianity out of expediency, Helena becomes a true believer (though we're not told how or why) and in old age submits to her vocation and embarks on the quest for which she is revered.

Evelyn considered *Helena* to be his best book. Not so reviewers, who had welcomed *The Loved One* as proof that he was back on track, and now had to think again. 'Mr Waugh is a powerful satirist but only a mediocre missionary,' was a typical comment. Evelyn's disappointment at its reception – it was 'like being jostled about in a crowd' – was compounded by a financial crisis. He and Laura were no longer stinking rich. They had been living way beyond their means and Laura, apparently unawares, had accumulated an overdraft of £6,400. To make matters worse the local tax inspector was dunning him for unpaid super-tax. 'I shall have to go to prison,' Evelyn told Nancy Mitford, 'but that is hell nowadays with wireless and lectures and psychiatry. Oh for the Marshalsea.'

Evelyn's preoccupation with style was not confined to his writing. It was part and parcel of the stately way he lived. Every morning his butler placed a copy of *The Times* by his bedside. Every evening he and Laura would dress for dinner. Should a male guest arrive without a dinner jacket, Evelyn would advise him to 'sack your man'. When in London he took a suite at the Hyde Park Hotel, a short taxi ride away from the Jesuit church at Farm Street, where he worshipped, and 'the small parish of St James's', which was home to White's and also to his tailor, hairdresser and shirtmaker. He drank champagne – 'the shortest road out of Welfaria' – as a matter of course and smoked Havana cigars. Cigars were now part of his act. They made for swagger, for emphasizing a point. 'Cigar in hand I become more boastful and ribald,' he admitted. And since, under Labour, the best cigars were virtually unobtainable, Evelyn got Peters to persuade his American agent to send them to him disguised as books (there were no sniffer dogs then).

In the interests of economy Evelyn eventually had to sack his 'man', as well as the other staff, but he continued to fill Piers Court with books, paintings and furniture, much of it bought on impulse after he'd had a few drinks. This expenditure was possible thanks to the 'Save the Children Fund', which had been drafted in such a way that Evelyn's acquisitions and the interests of his children, the fund's beneficiaries, always seemed to coincide. In other words, whatever he bought could usually be classified as 'an investment' on the children's behalf. Soon a large part of Evelyn's income went into this fund, thus minimizing his tax bill.[9] He also sold it some of his own possessions, like the manuscripts of his novels. The fund helped to keep him afloat until shortly before he died, at which point the Inland Revenue successfully challenged its tax-free status. But even then Peters somehow saw to it that his estate was only dunned for six years' back-taxes instead of the thirteen that was owed.

In July 1950, long overdue, Laura gave birth to Septimus, her seventh and last child. Evelyn, who as usual was absent, later told Bron that had they not been catholics, he and Laura would have stopped at three – which poses the question of how they stopped at seven, since Laura was only thirty-four. As devout Catholics they were forbidden to employ any form of contraception. That left abstinence. For Evelyn, at any rate, abstinence may have seemed less like an imposition than a convenient excuse for ceasing conjugal relations, since it's quite possible that by then he was not only losing interest in sex, but incapable of managing it. Although he was not yet fifty, he had been a heavy drinker for most of his adult life, only abstaining during Lent and for the three months he spent in Topusko. Furthermore, to combat his insomnia, he had begun to take large doses of chloral and bromide, the latter a byword among service personnel for suppressing sexual urges.

Bron Waugh said that his father's life was largely spent 'in the avoidance of boredom and of people who were likely to bore him'. This is the most charitable explanation for Evelyn's neglect of his children. Like Charles Ryder, whose wife has to remind him that while painting in South America he has acquired a daughter, Evelyn distanced himself from his offspring, regarding them as 'defective adults: feckless, destructive, frivolous, sensual, humourless'. Notoriously, he admitted in his wartime diary that he would rather lose four-year-old Bron to a V-bomb than the books he'd stored at the Hyde Park Hotel, because 'a child is easily replaced while a book destroyed is utterly lost'. (What price Arthur's lost library, about which he'd been so nonchalant?) A few years later, in a letter to Diana Cooper, he was a little more complimentary about them all: 'I am glad to possess them but get little pleasure from their use – like first editions.' But unlike first editions they were forbidden the library.

As the children grew up he began to take more notice of them, although the relationship was conducted on his terms. He reserved the right to withdraw his affection at a moment's notice – affection that was, in the case of his two eldest sons, in short supply anyway. He was more indulgent towards his daughters, particularly Meg for whom he conceived an almost incestuous passion. But this did not stop him from writing about her with the same 'brutal island frankness' (to borrow the phrase Nancy Mitford used of Randolph Churchill) that he employed with the others.

And yet... Apart from James, who said it was 'sheer hell' being his son, Evelyn's children, like his close friends, seem to have accepted that his good qualities, especially the way he made them laugh, outweighed the bad, and that it was understandable that he should regard them, in Bron's words, as 'part of the cross which every Christian must bear'. Bron did not even repine at his father's refusal to visit him in hospital in Cyprus, where he received the last rites following an accident with a machine gun while doing National Service. Evelyn had ceased keeping a diary by then and his letters do not explain why, unlike Laura, he chose to stay at home. Perhaps he was confident that having given so much to catholic charities, his prayers for Bron's survival – which we must assume he offered up – would be answered.

What Evelyn really thought about his family, or indeed anything personal except his religion, is a mystery of his own making. Enquiries about his inner life were as unwelcome as unannounced visitors to Piers Court, who had to brave a sign reading 'NO ADMITTANCE ON BUSINESS'. Even so experienced an interrogator as John Freeman got little change out of him during their television *tête-à-tête*. Evelyn's old comrade, Lord Birkenhead, said he hid his inmost thoughts behind an iron visor: 'It was as if he felt it would not only be grossly improper but also commonplace' to expose himself. Birkenhead supposed that he sometimes removed the mask when with family or close friends, and at confession. But all we have to go on are the diaries and letters, none of which was written on oath, and the testimony of Nancy Mitford that 'behind that mask of iron' there was 'real bonhomie'. It is true that like most novelists he sometimes gives himself away, but in retrospect even *The Ordeal of Gilbert Pinfold* is an affirmation rather than a revelation. Frances Donaldson, writing shortly after his death, described him as 'inimitable and inexplicable'. More than forty years and almost as many books later, that still seems just.

The Pinfold Years
1952–8

Nothing is so hideously uninteresting as an author with
a large family.

Edward Bulwer

On New Year's Day 1954 Duff Cooper died in his wife's arms.
Devastating though this was for Lady Diana, it removed the one
person who had always come between Evelyn and her.
Gradually they resumed their pre-war intimacy. 'You are never
long from my mind and never for a moment from my heart,'
wrote Evelyn. But they rarely met because he had neither the
energy nor the inclination to flit hither and thither like his rest-
less old flame. 'Your idea of friendship is to do things together;
mine is simply to be together,' he told her.

Evelyn saw even less of another old friend, Nancy Mitford,
who had settled in Paris after the war. Perhaps this was just as
well because her tongue was as sharp as his and there were certain things on which they could never agree, such as France, an
overrated country in Evelyn's opinion, and religion: 'I can't agree
that I must be debarred from ever mentioning your creator,' she
told him. 'Try to remember that he also created me.' Jokes were
what bound them together. 'We cherish our friends,' wrote
Evelyn, 'not for their ability to amuse us but for ours to amuse
them.' He and Nancy had always been on the same wavelength.
But living in France she no longer heard all the latest London

gossip. Having failed to persuade Cyril Connolly to become his 'pen-pal', Evelyn turned to Ian Fleming's wife, Ann, a shrewd, catty and well-informed *femme du monde* who told Evelyn what he wanted to hear and sometimes what he did not.

For instance he was always eager for news of people like Cyril Connolly and Peter Quennell, two of the leading 'fuddy-duddies', as he rather oddly called them, who frequented Mrs Fleming's salon. Evelyn would construct bizarre fantasies about them and their wives and 'concubines', a practice he began as an undergraduate in respect of Alec, whose premature baldness he ascribed to sexual excess. Ann, whose own marriage was far from conventional, fed these fantasies with a mixture of fact and fiction. But when, after reading *Officers and Gentlemen*, she mischievously identified Bob Laycock with the 'caddish' Ivor Claire, Evelyn gave notice on their 'beautiful friendship' should she ever mention this again: 'For Christ's sake lay off the idea of Bob = Claire … Just shut up about Laycock, Fuck You, E. Waugh.'

On paper, at any rate, Ann complied. But had she hit a nerve? Mark Amory, who edited her letters as well as Evelyn's, notes without comment that in his diary, Evelyn wrote that he had forbidden her to breathe a word of 'this cruel fact'.

Judged from a martial perspective, Evelyn's army career had been a disappointment. He ended the war as a captain, a poor return for five years in uniform. But judged from an artistic perspective it had been very rewarding indeed, allowing him to accumulate a large amount of literary capital that, properly invested, would reap substantial dividends. 'Men of other trades,' he reflected, 'called to the colours, are apt to feel that they have merely changed jobs for the worse. Any "job" is a change for the better to an artist for it gives him access to the source of his strength… In the army he gains experience which is hard to come by elsewhere.'

Sword of Honour, the savagely ironic title Evelyn chose for his military trilogy, is partly autobiographical. You have only to read his diaries to confirm this. But how much of it Evelyn had in his head before he began is hard to say, not least because about half-way through he went briefly mad, an experience recounted in *The Ordeal of Gilbert Pinfold*, which interrupts the sequence. Another puzzle concerns his hero, Guy Crouchback – though 'hero' seems inappropriate for someone whose ex-wife describes him, not unreasonably, as a 'wet, smug, obscene, pompous, sex-less lunatic pig'. Perhaps Evelyn thought she had a point, admitting to Anthony Powell that Guy was 'a prig', albeit 'a virtuous and brave prig'. At any rate as Graham Greene noted, Guy is 'curiously mislaid' in volumes two and three, appearing on less than a third of the pages. He is no longer the central consciousness, either.

Guy and Evelyn have much in common. They share the same birthday, the same faith and the same loathing for Stalin as well as for Hitler. They belong to the same club – called Bellamy's in the sequence – and they probably go to the same tailor and the same hairdresser. Their military careers are almost identical too. But they are not the same man. Evelyn was tuppence-coloured. Guy is penny-plain. He is also, by and large, a conformist. You can't imagine him telling a general where to get off. Presumably Evelyn intended him to be colourless, though it's not clear why. He could hardly argue, as he did with Charles Ryder, that the story isn't about him.

Guy is the last of the Crouchbacks, a landed recusant family with a direct line (they believe) to their Maker. Lonely, joyless and sterile, he has been languishing in Italy for several years when news of the Nazi-Soviet pact stiffens his sinews: 'The enemy at last was plain in view, huge and hateful, all disguise cast off. It was the Modern Age in arms. Whatever the outcome there was a place for him in that battle.' And much good does it do him, because before long the pass is sold, the cause dishonoured and victory, when it comes, has a bitter taste. But to begin with he is a happy warrior, enveloped in the bosom of the Royal Corps of Halberdiers.

Like the Royal Marines, on whom they are obviously based, the Halberdiers are not at all grand but brimming with *esprit de corps*, about which Evelyn is affectionately ironic. Guy is nick-named 'Uncle' on account of his advanced age, and exposed to the uncomplicated geniality of the Halberdiers' mess his po-face begins to crack. But try as he might Evelyn can't make Guy as interesting as three other halberdiers. One of these is the bat-talion black sheep, Trimmer, in civvy street a ladies' hairdresser. Trimmer is less a temporary gentleman than a permanent oik; but he's also a plausible rogue with sex appeal who consorts with Guy's ex-wife and is later reinvented as a bogus 'People's Hero'. But there's nothing bogus about the one-eyed brigadier, Ben Ritchie-Hook, a blunt instrument for whom tactics simply mean 'biffing', for which read smiting the enemy again and again until he succumbs. Finally there is the egregious Apthorpe – 'Uncle' Apthorpe, for he too is middle-aged like Guy. Apthorpe's an old bush hand. There's nothing you can't tell him about hygiene. That's why his most prized possession is his portable 'thunder box', a venerable Edwardian commode when using which Apthorpe always wears his tin helmet. This saves him from being brained by a booby-trap set by the brigadier, who covets the thun-der-box. But eventually he has to go because, as Evelyn explained to Nancy Mitford, he was threatening to take over the story.

Included in Evelyn's wartime diary is an enthralling account of his experiences in Crete, which he plundered for volume two, *Officers and Gentlemen*. Like Evelyn, Guy now belongs to a smart commando unit which is sent to act as rearguard for the evacua-tion of Crete. Much of what he sees appalls him, as it did Evelyn, in particular the conduct of two of his brother officers, Major 'Fido' Hound and Captain Ivor Claire. As we have heard, Major Hound, a punctilious staff officer who has no business being at the sharp end, is clearly drawn from life. But the identity of Ivor Claire, who disobeys orders and deserts his men, has never been established – if indeed he *was* drawn from life, as Ann Fleming supposed.

Wellington thought that dandies made the best soldiers and Claire, a blasé showjumper with an MC won at Dunkirk, seems to fit the bill. Guy reveres him as an old-fashioned upper-class hero, 'the fine flower of them all'. But there's a worm in the bud and Claire's defection marks the beginning of Guy's disillusionment with both the Army and the Allied cause. If the book has a hero – or anti-hero – it is Corporal-Major Ludovic, who takes command of the open boat in which Guy, whose men decline to join him, escapes. Guy owes his life to this sinister and inscrutable warrant officer, formerly the catamite of a creepy crypto-communist diplomat, who later, under the influence of 'that potent intoxicant, the English language', writes a trashy bestseller that exploits the same market for glossy pre-war nostalgia as *Brideshead*, which by then Evelyn had all but disowned.

Evelyn was a tidy writer and *Officers and Gentlemen* had plenty of loose ends, so readers must have been puzzled by his announcement that there would be no volume three. They were not to know that half half-way through writing the book, in January 1954, he had gone off his head and, as Graham Greene recalled, feared he might do so again. This did not happen, but the need to write about his ordeal while it was still fresh in his mind took precedence. He then very unselfishly offered to write the life of his moribund old friend, Monsignor Ronald Knox, a *beau geste* that occupied him fully for another eighteen months, at the end of which he was desperate for a holiday abroad. As usual Peters was able to cut a deal, but the quid pro quo, *A Tourist in Africa*, used up more time, so that five years had elapsed before he began work on volume three.

Gathering up the loose ends was a challenge to someone who could read the same detective story every six weeks and still wonder who the murderer was. He had to keep 'dipping in' to volumes one and two to find out what he'd written all those years before. A remark made by the painter Rex Whistler, who was killed in Normandy, crystallized the mood he sought to recapture. According to Diana Cooper, Whistler asked, 'What has victory got to do with it?' This, said Evelyn, was the very question he longed to hear in the last years of the war. Not hearing it made him morose. 'It is the theme of my own little trilogy.'

After a prologue, in which Guy learns that his father is dying, *Unconditional Surrender* opens with a description of the crowds queuing outside Westminster Abbey to see the Sword of Stalingrad. Guy, whose fortieth birthday it is, averts his gaze from this base homage. What he cannot ignore, however, is that unless some miracle occurs he will end the war as unfulfilled as he began it, having failed to secure a place in the battle. It is not the same battle, of course, since Russia joined the Allies, but Guy would still like to do his bit, if only to atone for all the advantages he has enjoyed. But danger, he belatedly recognizes, does not necessarily justify privilege and the age of miracles is past. In Yugoslavia, his final posting, a Jewish couple he has befriended are compromised by his interest in them and probably shot, so ending any hopes he might have had of making the world a better place. Ironically it is thanks to his ex-wife, Virginia, whose infidelity unmanned him, that Guy is able to perform a chivalrous act. Virginia conceives a baby by the unspeakable Trimmer, gives birth, and is promptly and providentially killed by a bomb. Guy, who has never ceased to think of her as his wife, agrees to raise little Trimmer as his son and heir. Holy water, in his eyes, is thicker than blood.

Evelyn's friend Anthony Powell used to say that with even the best novelists there is always something you have to put up with. For many readers of *Sword of Honour* that something is the Crouchback family, whom Virginia derides as 'over-bred and under-sexed'. Tough, outspoken and amoral, like the hostesses Evelyn adored in real life, Virginia is one of the many vital characters who more than make up for the Crouchbacks' lack of zest. Another bonus is Evelyn's description of the Cretan debacle, which has been compared to Hemingway's account of Caporetto in *A Farewell to Arms*. His social observation is also excellent. For instance the contrast between the unsmart but absolutely reliable halberdiers and the stylish, but equivocal grandees in the commandos is spot on. Despite his disenchantment with the war and its aftermath, army life with its customs and exigencies continued to fascinate him. And according to another temporary officer, the writer and academic Goronwy Rees, the way he captured 'the essence of that experience' was exemplary:

> The extraordinary combination of boredom with moments of intense excitement; the sense of being thrust into an entirely strange and novel world, at once barbaric and yet intensely traditional; the atmosphere of total confusion, the triumph of the arbitrary, created by exact and meticulous observation of elaborate and frequently absurd regulations; the unnerving oscillations between tragedy and farce – all these Waugh has observed with impeccable accuracy, and any future historian of the British Army will have to take his observations into account.

Two distinguished historians, A.J. P. Taylor and Eric Hobsbawm, neither of whom belonged on the same side of the barricades as Evelyn, endorsed Goronwy Rees's verdict. It is also worth noting that in postulating communist machinations in high places Evelyn was not as preposterously wide of the mark as his detractors then supposed.

Terence Greenidge said that at Oxford Evelyn reminded him of 'a rogueish cherub'. By 1947, when Osbert Lancaster executed his striking caricature of a bowler-hatted Evelyn, cigar in hand, 'confronting the age of the common man' on the steps of White's, the cherub had long since yielded to the goblin. 'Mr Waugh, who gives pleasure to so many, seldom looks pleased,' noted an American. The 'common man' was not wholly to blame. Evelyn had begun to suffer from a chronic metaphysical hangover, that dispiriting condition, 'incomparably more dreadful' than its physical counterpart, that Kingsley Amis adumbrates in his handbook *On Drink*. If this sounds fanciful, Evelyn's post-war diaries exhibit the very symptoms that Amis itemizes, that 'ineffable compound of depression, sadness, anxiety, self-hatred, sense of failure and fear for the future'.

Funnily enough Amis recommends reading Chesterton's *Lepanto*, a favourite poem of Evelyn's, by way of an antidote. But another of his suggestions, listening to music, would have been no use at all. Evelyn was not only tone deaf; he despised music. It was one of the reasons he loathed 'the wireless'. Since he also shunned country pursuits and made no attempt to mix with his neighbours, whom he supposed, probably correctly, would bore him, he had plenty of time to kill when he wasn't working. In early days at Piers Court he had gardened and taken long walks, but after the war, increasingly beset by aches and pains, he took less and less exercise. Two or three times a week he went to the local cinema at Dursley, regardless of what was showing. He must, he thought, have seen more bad films than any living man.

One pair of neighbours who were welcome at Piers Court were the biographer Frances Donaldson and her husband Jack, a Labour MP, later Minister for the Arts, who had a small dairy farm like Laura's. Lady Donaldson described herself as belonging to the 'no-man's-land between the smart and the intellectual' and this could explain her attraction for Evelyn who liked, she wrote, 'the smarter of the intellectuals, the more intellectual of the smart'. Like some of Attlee's cabinet the Donaldsons combined socialist principles with upper-class credentials: they had a flat in Albany and a son at Eton, where Jack had been. Another recommendation was that they both knew and admired P.G. Wodehouse, whose biography Frances Donaldson later wrote. Once Jack had passed the sartorial test for dinner chez Waugh – he wore a black tie the first time they dined there – their card was marked and they became frequent visitors. One happy consequence of this was Frances Donaldson's intimate portrait of Evelyn as a country neighbour, in which his charm, so often overlooked, is emphasized. Charm, like stimulating talk, is difficult to convey on paper but there is no reason to disbelieve Frances Donaldson when she says that Evelyn possessed it in abundance – 'the most charming, enchanting, absolutely outstandingly lovely man I ever met.' She also mentions his 'light, fruity voice' (not unlike John Gielgud's in the part of Ryder's father on television), quite different from the bark that might have been expected, and his habit of serving short drinks in very large glasses, so you began proceedings with the equivalent of a triple.

Evelyn was a generous host, but unpredictable. There was always an element of 'feasting with panthers' when dining with him. A mistake people sometimes made, understandable but inexcusable in Evelyn's eyes, was to praise him to his face. Even Lady Donaldson, who as the daughter of Freddie Lonsdale, a successful pre-war playwright, knew how crass fans could be, was surprised at the hostility he sometimes displayed towards adulation. Just as he expected conversation to be conducted along the rigorous lines he considered appropriate, so it was not enough to come out with some uninformed compliment, however sincerely meant. Comments had to be 'pointed and particular', otherwise the speaker could expect to be roughed up like the hapless American woman mentioned in the Preface.

The Donaldsons were unusual in that they became Laura's friends as well. They all went on holiday together, considered a very rash move, and it was to the Donaldsons that Laura turned when she realized from his letters that Evelyn, on a cruise to Colombo, was in a bad way. Then, apparently quite out of the blue, Evelyn surrendered to his besetting sin and said something unforgiveable about Freddie Lonsdale. The fable of the scorpion and the frog comes to mind. Like the scorpion, Evelyn couldn't help himself; it was in his nature, an example of the 'ineradicable caddishness' that he shared with heroes of his like Basil Seal and *The Loved One*'s Dennis Barlow. Afterwards Lady Donaldson acknowledged that his slur might not have been spontaneous but consequential. Perhaps she had begun to bore Evelyn, or unwittingly done something to offend him. But she did not dare to ask because there was the 'hideous risk' he might tell her – in 'lacerating' detail.

Evelyn's low spirits were matched by his physical decline. He was going deaf in one ear and was plagued by rheumatism, which became so bad at the end of 1953 that for a time he needed two sticks to get about. And, as always, there was his insomnia. When spending the night at Piers Court Lady Violet Powell smelt fresh cigar smoke at 4 a.m., which she took to be evidence of Evelyn's 'insomniac ramblings'. He had not had a good night's sleep in years and, like Rossetti, was ingesting chloral in 'fabulous quantities', with equally alarming results. 'My memory is not at all hazy,' he told John Betjeman, '– just sharp, detailed and dead wrong.' Betjeman soon had proof of this. For Evelyn's fiftieth birthday he gave him an elaborate Victorian wash-hand stand they had both admired at a friend's house. Evelyn thanked him for this but said that either there was an important piece missing or he'd misremembered its appearance. He *had* misremembered. Worse was to come.

Piers Court was not a cosy place to be in the depths of winter, particularly if you suffered from aches and pains. In January 1954, as was his wont, Evelyn took ship for warmer climes, his destination Colombo, in Ceylon. Since he always slept better at sea he took only 'the dregs' of his usual sleeping draught, but it was soon apparent to Laura that all was far from well. He wrote to say that he was the victim of a whispering campaign which he could overhear through the ship's ventilation system and that there were some 'psychologists' aboard who were able to read his mind through 'malevolent telepathy'. He insisted he wasn't 'balmy' (sic) or suffering from persecution mania and that once he'd returned he would seek out 'a rival telepathist' to ward them off.

In fact it was neither a telepathist nor an exorcist (his next idea) who cured Evelyn but an eminent catholic psychiatrist, Dr

Eric Strauss, whom he saw at the insistence of his friend Father Philip Caraman, editor of the Jesuit periodical *Month*. Dr Strauss concluded that the mocking voices he'd heard were aural hallucinations brought about by ingesting chloral and bromide on top of alcohol, the very cocktail that had done for Rossetti. This diagnosis was confirmed by a specialist. Mightily relieved to learn that he was neither going mad nor possessed by devils Evelyn resolved to follow Dr Strauss' advice and write an account of his ordeal – what Tom Driberg described as 'do it yourself shock therapy'. But he did not do as the specialist advised and give up barbiturates. Instead he obtained a prescription for paraldehyde – less destructive to a heavy drinker than chloral and bromide, but to be treated with caution because, like alcohol, it was a depressant. Evelyn did not treat it with caution and it must have aggravated the melancholia that was such a feature of his last years.

It took Evelyn several weeks to recover from his 'madness', which he never sought to disguise. He then applied himself to finishing *Officers and Gentlemen*, which was long overdue. This task was completed by mid-November, allowing him to clear the decks and unpack, like his alter ego Gilbert Pinfold, the hamper of 'fresh, rich experience' he had brought back from his traumatic cruise. Then he learnt that his mother, who had been poorly for some time, had died at the age of eighty-four. Although he had supported her financially since Arthur's death, such visits as he had paid her had been strictly dutiful, hence the remorse he felt at withholding from her the 'affection and attention' she deserved. He had adored her when young but found her less and less tolerable as the years went by. Her death, he said, was a 'happy release' – for him, it must be supposed, as well as for her.

Mr Pinfold, named in honour of the family who once owned Piers Court, sits down to describe his ordeal as soon as he gets the all-clear from his doctor. Not so Evelyn, who could only manage a rough outline during the two months break he took in Jamaica at the beginning of 1955. But in view of the controversies in which he would soon be embroiled now seems the moment to quote from the disobliging self-portrait with which the story opens:

His strongest tastes were negative. He abhorred plastics, Picasso, sunbathing, and jazz – everything in fact that had happened in his own lifetime. The tiny kindling of charity which came to him through his religion sufficed only to temper his disgust and change it to boredom... Shocked by a bad bottle of wine, an impertinent stranger, or a fault in syntax, his mind like a cinema camera trucked furiously forward to confront the offending object close-up with glaring lens... He offered the world a front of pomposity mitigated by indiscretion, that was as hard, bright and antiquated as a cuirass.

'What need we any further witness?' asked his enemies, who ranged from combative High Tory sceptics like the Oxford don Hugh Trevor-Roper, with whom he had already had an acri-monious exchange on the meaning of the word 'recusant', to angry young upstarts like John Wain and Kingsley Amis, always spelt 'Ames' by Evelyn. Evelyn answered these critics in kind. He also gave as good as he got when three interviewers from the BBC tried to bait him (asked whether, as an advocate of capital punishment, he would be prepared to hang someone himself, he said it would be very odd if they chose a novelist for such a specialized task). But in response to sniping from Lord Beaverbrook's papers he looked for more reward than the last word, hoping, as he told Peters, to catch one of them in libel.

Although there is no proof that Beaverbrook himself selected Evelyn as a target, Evelyn believed this to be the case. 'Of course I believe in the Devil,' he said. 'How else would I account for the existence of Lord Beaverbrook?' What particularly irked him was the *ad hominem* nature of the pieces, which purported to be reviews, but were as much about the author as the book. For instance, discussing *Officers and Gentlemen* in the *Sunday Express*, Robert Pitman reported that beneath Evelyn's coat of arms were the words *Industria Ditat* – Hard Work Makes You Rich, an appropriate motto, he considered for a self-made man who began life in Golders Green. A few weeks later the star *Express* columnist Nancy Spain, accompanied by an eccentric Labour Peer, Lord Noel-Buxton, were sent packing by Evelyn when they tried to interview him at Piers Court, having been told on the phone that they would not be welcome. He sent them packing again in the *Spectator* and followed this up by reporting, in another piece, that a recent survey had concluded that the Beaverbrook Press no longer had any influence at all on the sale of books.

Nancy Spain was the lead book reviewer on the *Express*, so of course this cut her to the quick. Beaverbrook was equally annoyed and probably encouraged her to take the line she did, which was to attack Evelyn – 'There is a war between Evelyn Waugh and me' – by comparing him unfavourably with Alec, who after years in the doldrums had written a bestseller, *Island in the Sun*, which even before publication had earned him more money from film and serial rights than his countless other books put together. Ms Spain, who had puffed Alec's book, claimed much of the credit for this. But she also said that Alec's first-edition sales dwarfed Evelyn's and implied that there was bad blood between them. This gave Evelyn the opening he needed, but to exploit it fully he would need Alec to be on side.

Alec had always acknowledged his brother's genius, but it must have been galling for him to be reminded of it at this particular juncture. A few years before, having lost the knack of writing short stories for bountiful American magazines like *The Saturday Evening Post*, he had contemplated suicide. Now, back in the limelight, he was being asked to share it with someone who for years had belittled him. But share it he did. By testifying on

Evelyn's behalf he gave the lie to any suggestion of bad blood between them and he also stated that first-edition sales were not necessarily the gauge of a book's success: before the war publishers deliberately did a small first print run so that they could announce that they were reprinting before the book went on sale. Although Evelyn himself was uncharacteristically hesitant in the witness box – at one point he would have 'settled for a fiver' he told Nancy Mitford – the jury found for him and he was awarded £2,000 – tax-free – plus costs.

Meanwhile another *Express* writer, Anthony Hern, had made the mistake of quoting a defamatory statement about Evelyn when reviewing a new edition of Rebecca West's *The Meaning of Treason*. Dame Rebecca, in ancient days one of Beaverbrook's mistresses, said that Evelyn and Graham Greene had fostered an intellectual climate in which treason could flourish. Greene chose to ignore this. Not so Evelyn, who scented blood. Reluctant to take money off Dame Rebecca, who had praised his work in the past, Evelyn sued her publisher, Pan Books, and the *Express*. Pan caved in immediately, pulping all unsold copies of the book, and agreeing to pay Evelyn's costs. The *Express* also settled out of court, but in addition to Evelyn's costs they paid him a further £3,000 tax-free in damages.

* * *

Evelyn had other worries besides lawsuits, beginning with his children. Some of them had inherited his subversive streak and as they grew up they became less biddable. Their education, which cost him dear, did not proceed smoothly. Bron was constantly in trouble at Downside and Meg and Hatty were no happier at their convents. Only Teresa, who became head girl and won a scholarship to Oxford, seems to have enjoyed boarding school. Her reward was a London Season, the expense of which was not made easier for Evelyn to bear by the disturbing sight of so many men in dinner jackets instead of tails at her coming-out ball; they included grandees like the Duke of Devonshire who should, Evelyn thought, have known better.

Another concern was the spread of Dursley, in which were to be found a rubber goods factory and a large engineering works. Evelyn feared they would soon be surrounded by housing estates; it was time to move. In August 1956 Piers Court was sold for £9,500 (in 2010 it went for £2.5 million!). Soon afterwards they bought Combe Florey House, not far from Pixton Park in Somerset, for £7,500. A 'cosy and secluded' mansion in red sandstone, dating from 1675 but enlarged in the eighteenth century, it included a medieval archway gatehouse where Evelyn hoped in vain to site a private chapel and enough land for Laura to graze her cows. Evelyn's libel suits had not yet been resolved and he had to borrow £2,000 for repairs and refurbishments. When the damages were awarded he astonished everyone, including the makers – who urged him to reconsider – by spending another £2,000 on a copy of a garish Wilton carpet exhibited at the 1851 Exhibition.

Soon after they had settled in at Combe Florey Evelyn corrected the proofs of *Pinfold*, which was published in June. Both Anthony Powell and Graham Greene thought this was one of his finest books, but its reception elsewhere was decidedly mixed, not least because thanks to the self-portrait with which it opened the temptation to review the man, rather than the book, was almost irresistible. Someone who took this line – in an article, not a review – was the bestselling author, J.B. Priestley, one of the architects, it was popularly supposed, of Labour's victory in 1945. Answering the question, 'What Was Wrong With Pinfold?', he said it was a case of mistaken identity. Pinfold was a novelist posing as a Catholic landed gentleman and not, as he would have you believe, a Catholic landed gentleman who happened to write novels. If he persisted in this delusion he would surely go off his head again, drugs or no drugs, since the two roles were incompatible. This was the sort of piece that made Evelyn 'eat the carpet' and he retaliated fiercely, accusing

Priestley of 'sucking-up' to the lower classes who had repaid his faith in them by spending their days off visiting stately homes instead of queueing for avant-garde plays.

Evelyn's friends, who regarded Priestley as a humbug, thought he had the better of this exchange. But his image, stylized to a degree, did him no favours at a time when, as in the Twenties, social barriers were beginning to crumble. Invariably photographed in a heavy three-piece suit and smoking a cigar, he had recently acquired yet another prop, a two-foot-long Victorian ear trumpet which he would ostentatiously remove from his deaf ear to indicate that he was bored. According to Evelyn's cousin Claud Cockburn, the trumpet was also meant to emphasise 'the laborious difficulty its owner had in understanding any communication the modern world might be seeking to make to him'. Typically he joined Nancy Mitford in the wide-ranging debate about U and non-U usage, deploring the 'new wave of philistinism' resulting from the 'free distribution of university degrees to the deserving poor' and pronouncing birth control 'flagrantly middle-class'. It may have been a tease, like his suggestion that women smoking in the streets should be placed under arrest. But then again it may not. In *Basil Seal Rides Again*, Evelyn's last work of fiction, Basil ruefully concludes that the part of an old buffer he had adopted in jest has taken over: 'the parody had become the *persona*'. Ann Fleming, to whom this short story was dedicated, had already concluded that Evelyn had 'developed a personality which he hates, but cannot escape from'.

And yet, despite his regret that the Conservative government had failed to turn back the clock at all, he was not an identikit Blimp. The Empire, an essentially protestant enterprise, meant little to him. He minded the bombing of Bath more than the fall of Singapore, believed that the Suez expedition could not be justified on either legal or moral grounds and thought that in Southern Africa the whites, British as well as Boer, had treated the blacks shamefully. Nor did he set his face against *all* modern art: he had the brilliant idea of using one of Francis Bacon's paintings for the cover of *Pinfold*, but it fell through.

Another quality of Evelyn's that deserves to be recorded is his generosity towards new writers. In the case of his old friend Alfred Duggan this was understandable (much later, when in poor health himself, he was instrumental in setting up a fund for Duggan's widow and adopted son). But no ties bound him to Angus Wilson, whose *Hemlock and After* he acclaimed, or Sybille Bedford, whose 'remarkable historical novel' *A Legacy* delighted him. He was also one of the first to praise Muriel Spark, V.S. Naipaul and Eric Newby. Strangely, given the hero's subversive qualities, Waugh found nothing to admire in *Lucky Jim*. Perhaps Jim's 'Evelyn Waugh face' was a tease too far. What he could not have foreseen was that forty years on people would disparage Amis in the same terms that they disparaged him. For instance Amis once complained that for twenty minutes he'd sat at the bar of the Garrick club 'and nobody came near me'. His companion replied, 'Kingsley, doesn't it strike you that it could be because you can be so fucking *curmudgeonly*?' Something similar happened to Evelyn at White's. 'Why are you alone?' asked a fellow member. 'Because no one wants to speak to me.' 'I can tell you exactly why; because you sit there on your arse looking like a stuck pig.'

Change and Decay
1961–6

Only when one has lost all curiosity about the future has
one reached the age to write an autobiography.

Evelyn Waugh

By moving to Somerset Evelyn became a distant neighbour of
Anthony Powell, with whom he was now on good terms again
following a long estrangement caused by Powell's friendship
with John Heygate and She-Evelyn. Evelyn admired Powell's
A Dance to the Music of Time sequence, to see the completion of
which was, he said, one of the few reasons he had to desire
longevity. But when in 1956 Powell became a CBE, Evelyn's
letter of congratulation ('I should rather like something of the
sort myself') concealed his belief that in accepting 'this degrad-
ing decoration' (as he described it to Nancy Mitford) Powell had
let the side down. A writer, he believed, should settle for nothing
less than a knighthood or a CH, preferably the former, to obtain
which, he told Christopher Sykes, he would lick the Prime
Minister's boots.

Three years later he felt that the prize was within his reach
following the cordial relations he had established with Prime
Minister Harold Macmillan, one of the primary sources for his
biography of Mgr Ronald Knox. So it came as a crushing blow
when he learnt that all he could hope for was the CBE, a bauble
he had no hesitation in refusing. Later he regretted his 'side',

which probably cost him any further honours (prime ministers, like God, are not mocked). But it is worth noting that his old adversary, J.B. Priestley, having turned down a knighthood and a peerage, was awarded the Order of Merit. Had Evelyn lived longer he too might have been forgiven. When, in March 1963, he was invited to become a Companion (C. Litt.) by the Royal Society of Literature, he accepted; even though it lacked cachet he thought it would be 'stuck up' to refuse.

Mgr Knox, who moved, as Maurice Bowra put it, in 'the same circle of well-situated catholic converts' as Evelyn, also became the Waughs' neighbour when they moved to Somerset – but only briefly: he had incurable cancer, news his doctors concealed from him for many months. Charitably – for he was trying to polish off *Pinfold* – Evelyn agreed to accompany him on a 'rest-cure', in reality a 'ghastly' rain-sodden fortnight among the genteel geriatrics of Torquay and Sidmouth, after which Evelyn invited Knox for another two weeks' convalescence at Combe Florey. Enveloped in smoke from his smelly pipe as he wrestled with the *Times* crossword (which he made more difficult by read-ing only the across clues), and played endless games of Scrabble, Knox, once regarded as the wittiest clergyman since Sydney Smith, was not an inspiring companion. That Evelyn should have sat so long with him makes his subsequent refusal to per-form the same office for Bron seem even more contrary, partic-ularly since proximity to Knox seems to have reopened social wounds. When Anthony Powell remarked that he was 'never at any moment conscious of the stiffness and reserve' that some of Knox's obituaries referred to, Evelyn replied, 'You were at Eton and Balliol.'

Knox died in August 1957, whereupon Evelyn set to work on his biography, an absorbing task he would complete in just eighteen months – 'Ronnie's death has transformed my life', he told Diana Cooper. 'Instead of sitting about bored and idle I am busy all day long…' His researches took him as far as Rhodesia, where the son of his hostess recalled his 'infectious laugh' and habit of drinking beer at breakfast, something he hadn't done since Oxford. But there was nothing remotely Bacchanalian about the work he produced, which must have disappointed those who recalled the lively appreciation of Knox he wrote for *Horizon*. That, however, was a secular piece, about the writer rather than the priest. The reverse is true of the biography, an act of *pietas* in which very few of the amusing anecdotes associated with Knox are quoted. He comes across as a rather sombre figure, unrecognizable as the wit to whom, as Evelyn once put it, 'all epigrams are attributed'.

No sooner had Evelyn corrected the proofs of *Knox* than he took his usual winter break, this time in East and Central Africa, where the winds of change were beginning to blow. Not that these troubled him. He had a very jolly time – too jolly, in fact, because as he later explained to one of his hostesses, 'I can only be funny when I am complaining about something.' Committed to writing a 'potboiler' with plenty of publicity for his benefactors, the Union Castle shipping line, he was reduced to expedients like ridiculing the dress of colonial officials. In their white shorts and shirts they looked, he thought, like 'grotesquely overgrown little boys who have not yet qualified for the first eleven at their private schools'. More contentiously he was unimpressed by the achievements of the 'Great White Chief', Cecil Rhodes: 'He was a visionary and almost all he saw was hallucination.' Nor would this exchange, with a boastful local bigwig, have pleased the settlers either:

> I said: 'I think you are a bachelor. I should not care to bring up children here.'
> 'Why not?' rather sharply scenting politics.
> 'The accent.'

Evelyn's opinion of *A Tourist in Africa* may be gauged by the blurb, which he must have written himself. '[This] travel diary makes a very pleasant bed-side book (which should induce sleep in all but the most stubborn insomniacs.)'

For much of the time Evelyn was writing *Knox* his son Bron was being painstakingly patched up following his accident with a machine gun in Cyprus, where he had been serving with Evelyn's old regiment, the Blues. Bron had six bullet wounds and was incredibly lucky to survive, losing his spleen, one lung, several ribs, a finger, '*but nothing else*'.[10] Invalided out of the army he occupied himself before going up to Oxford by writing a mordant autobiographical novel, *The Foxglove Saga*, which Evelyn described as 'bizarre' but 'very funny'. He and Bron were now on better terms, though Bron chafed at his dependency. Like Evelyn he had won an award at Oxford; unlike Evelyn he soon tired of the place and left after a year to pursue a very successful career in Grub Street.

Teresa, meanwhile, had fallen in love with John d'Arms, the 'penniless' American classical scholar whom she would later marry. That still left four children to be fed and watered, to say nothing of Laura's cows which cost, Evelyn reckoned, 'as much to keep as a troupe of ballet dancers'. The cows were got rid off at the end of 1960, as were the Italian couple who had looked after the Waughs since the other servants were culled. Evelyn now struggled to earn half as much, in real terms, as he had in 1938. He had to be hard-nosed about his journalism. In a letter of refusal to a young editor soliciting a contribution to his magazine he explained the 'predicament' of a middle-aged writer like himself, forced to chose between the popular press and small magazines like the editor's:

> In the first case he will find his work mutilated by sub-editors and scrawled over with inappropriate titles, but he will be paid 20 times as much as by a more humane employer. The choice is between vanity and avarice. The avarice is not always selfish. Elderly men have many dependants. They

are not to be blamed severely if they choose to sacrifice their vanity.

Evelyn restated this principle when interviewed by John Freeman for the BBC Television programme, *Face to Face*. After repeatedly failing to get a rise out of him Freeman managed to establish that he would rather be ignored than not. Then why, asked Freeman, have you agreed to appear on this programme? 'Poverty,' answered Evelyn. 'We've both been hired to talk in this deliriously happy way.'

Teresa and John d'Arms were married in June 1961. A month later, after a brief engagement, it was Bron's turn. Like his father he was 'marrying up': his fiancée, the Honourable Teresa Onslow, was the daughter of an earl. Although Evelyn grumbled at the expense, the prospect of American grandchildren and Teresa Onslow's refusal to become a catholic, he did not repine at his two eldest flying the nest. But when, the following year, Meg announced that she had found Mr Right, he was heart-broken. A few months before they'd had a lovely time together in the West Indies and British Guiana; now she was lost to him. 'Little Meg is ripe for the kind of love I can't give her,' he admitted to Diana Cooper. 'So I am surrendering with the honours of war – without war indeed.' He derived some comfort from knowing that her fiancé, Giles FitzHerbert, was a gentleman and a catholic. But in other respects, he told Nancy Mitford, he was not the sort of suitor 'an old fashioned father would have preferred', possessing no obvious merits.

Photographed with Meg on her wedding day Evelyn wore his 'stuck-pig' face. He wore a braver face in *Basil Seal Rides Again*, the short tale he wrote in response to Meg's betrothal. Having had an even more futile war than Evelyn's, Basil has married his wealthy mistress, Angela Lyne, and lived off her contentedly ever since. Then his beloved daughter Barbara brings home a raffish boyfriend in whom Basil sees a disturbing resemblance to himself when young. Consumed with jealousy as well as concern for Barbara's welfare he convinces her that he is the impudent young rotter's father, a stratagem denied to Evelyn himself, and so blights her hopes.

Most reviewers, unaware of Evelyn's anguish over Meg, agreed that both he and his hero could still put one over their juniors. But Nancy Mitford, with her intimate knowledge of Basil's progenitor, objected that 'Prod has turned into you and this falsifies everything'. However rich Basil might now be, he would never have become so hidebound as to quibble over incest – 'Or was he meant to be jealous? If so we are in deep water indeed.' Evelyn confirmed that Basil *was* jealous, but insisted he wasn't the boyfriend's father. Nancy, noting the features they shared, said this was rot. Anthony Powell was even more dis-obliging. Admitting that he'd never cared for Basil, he said he hoped there would be a further instalment 'in which you kill him off in painful circumstances'. He hoped in vain. Evelyn's career as a novelist was over. He was now writing *A Little Learning*, the first of a projected three volumes of autobiography that would bring in, said Peters, '£5,000 a year for six years'.

It was about now that Evelyn told Diana Cooper his 'ghastly brother' had written an autobiography (*The Early Years of Alec Waugh*) in which he said, 'Venus has been kind to me'. He included no such boasts in *A Little Learning*, which had it not contained a passage in which 'Captain Grimes' describes how he had his wicked way with 'Knox minor', could safely have been read by his maiden aunts. So 'decorous' was his manner that Angus Wilson, writing after Evelyn's death, doubted whether 'Waugh the biographer' could ever have done justice to a per-sonality as 'splendid' as his own. He thought 'the ghost of his father had returned to possess him and force him to mend his literary ways'.

However that might be Evelyn did acknowledge, for the first time, his debt to Arthur – not just for his forbearance, but also for something he had often disparaged, his literary legacy.

Hearing him read aloud from the works of his favourite novelists and poets Evelyn assimilated the riches of the English language, an inheritance that found its way into everything he wrote. 'Some people,' he told an interviewer, 'think in pictures, some in ideas. I think entirely in words.'

Losing Meg was not the only trauma Evelyn suffered as he approached his sixtieth birthday. Thanks to Ann Fleming he learnt that the Governor-General of the West Indies and his wife, with whom he and Meg stayed en route to British Guiana, had found him 'a frightful bore'. When Nancy Mitford assured him that his hosts were at fault, not him, and that it was unforgiveable of Ann to pass on this calumny, he said the 'crucial point' was that he thought that he'd charmed and delighted them. Failure to realize that you were boring someone was an appalling predicament: 'I can never go out again.'

But neither Meg's marriage nor his fear of becoming a bore agitated Evelyn half as much as *aggiornamento*, the process by which, following the Second Vatican Council, his Church sought to move with the times. He wanted no part of Ecumenicism, declaring that catholicism was the enemy of (Roman) Catholicism. Still less did he welcome the ditching of the Latin liturgy in favour of the vernacular, a measure designed to make the mass more meaningful and inclusive for the congregation. His despair at these changes was profound, particularly once it became apparent that whatever reservations they might express in private, the Catholic hierarchy in Britain would not rock the boat. A year before he died he wrote, 'Pray God I will never apostasize but I can only now go to church as an act of duty and obedience.'

Evelyn's mood cannot have been improved by the knowledge that in the next volume of his autobiography, provisionally entitled *A Little Hope*, he would have to write about his first marriage. When Christopher Sykes, nervous about how he would be treated in volume two, tried to draw him out, Evelyn sighed and said he had no cause for alarm: 'No one has. I wish they had. My life is roughly speaking over. I sleep badly except occasionally in the morning. I get up late. I try to read my letters. I try to read the paper. I have some gin. I try to read the paper again. I have some more gin. I try to think about my autobiography. Then I have some more gin and it's lunch time. That's my life. It's ghastly.'

Diana Cooper thought that if only he could regain his appetite all would be well. His teeth were so bad that eating was a painful chore; but their removal without anaesthetic, referred to above, enfeebled him further. Nor did he ever come to terms with dentures. 'We live off boiled eggs and tinned turtle soup,' he reported. His diary, now little more than occasional jottings, contains mournful reflections such as: 'Re-reading Robert Byron. It was fun thirty-five years ago to travel far and in great discomfort to meet people whose entire conception of life and manner of expression were alien. Now one has only to leave one's gates.' Beneath this is the stark pronouncement, 'All fates are "worse than death".'

Evelyn had posed as a doddery old buffer for so long that only his family and closest friends were aware how decrepit he really was. In November 1965 Anthony Powell and his wife met the Waughs at a country wedding. Evelyn seemed at once 'portly, yet wasted'. He was shaky on his pins – so shaky, in fact, that he needed help to ascend the modest ramp that led from the marquee in which the reception was held to the lawn above. As both couples left Evelyn gave a feeble wave. It proved to be Powell's last glimpse of him.

The changes in the liturgy meant that it was now rare for Evelyn to hear the mass said in Latin. On Easter Day 1966, thanks to his friend Father Caraman, who was staying with the Waughs, Evelyn enjoyed this privilege. Afterwards a large party assembled at Combe Florey House for lunch. Evelyn was in good spirits, even managing a warm welcome for Laura's brother Auberon. At some point before the meal he disappeared and could not at first be found. Then someone noticed that the downstairs lavatory was occupied. Evelyn had had a massive heart attack while straining at stool, a death that evoked Apthorpe and his thunder box, as Graham Greene, among others, noted. He was buried in the grounds of the house, within sight of the tiny parish church where Sydney Smith had been rector, and granted a requiem mass ten days later at Westminster Cathedral. Grudgingly, the hierarchy allowed the Latin rite to be followed. They also permitted the singing of 'O God our help in ages past' – The Old Hundredth – a traditional Anglican hymn derived from the psalm sung by his men at the burial of John Hampden.[10] Recalling the 'preposterous' use to which these stirring lines were put in *Decline and Fall* Christopher Sykes wondered if this wasn't Evelyn's last joke. Bron Waugh demurred. It was, he said, a concession to the very many Anglicans, outnumbering catholics, who were present. If this was the case, then the joke was on Evelyn.

Legacy

Like Kipling, the subject of one of his last reviews, Evelyn received some offhand obituaries. This was partly because, as A.D. Peters wrote in his letter of condolence to Laura, 'the world who did not know him had, I'm afraid, a distorted picture of him that he himself took some trouble to paint'. But it was also because, like Kipling, he belonged to a world that had had its day. Coincidentally, the week after Evelyn died *Time* magazine, owned by his erstwhile benefactors, the Luce family, published its effusive 'Swinging London' issue, a celebration of the 'alien' manners and morals he had glimpsed beyond his gates. From that perspective his death had come not a moment too soon. He was also spared senility, something he had dreaded.

Evelyn always said he never saved a penny and the modest sum he left, approximately £20,000 gross, seemed to confirm this. In fact many of his assets had long since gone to the Save the Children Fund; nor did his wealth at death reflect either the value of his literary estate or of his magnificent library, which included a superlative collection of Victorian illustrated books bought at bargain prices before the war. But Laura, misled by her advisers as to the amount of back tax that was owed in addition to death duties, imagined she was destitute. Rather than sell the house – though for a time it was on the market – she asked her son-in-law, John D'Arms, to try and find an American buyer for the library. After lengthy negotiations the whole bang shoot –

shelves, furniture, carpets and ornaments, in addition to the thousands of books and assorted manuscripts – was sold to the University of Texas for £30,000, far less than it would have realized had items been sold individually, or even in lots, but considerably more than the 'song' referred to by Bron.

After Evelyn's death neither Laura nor Bron could bring themselves to read his diaries, which went to Texas with everything else. In December 1972 a xeroxed copy of them arrived on Peters' desk from Texas, for forwarding to Evelyn's authorized biographer, Christopher Sykes. Peters, who died shortly afterwards, realized their potential and offered them to the *Sunday Times*, whose literary editor, Leonard Russell, after what can only have been a cursory examination, advised against a bid. His advice was not taken and an offer of £6,000 for serialization rights was made. Meanwhile the diaries had arrived at the *Observer*, whose literary editor, Terry Kilmartin, passed them on to his colleague, Michael Davie. It did not take Davie long to conclude that there was gold amidst the dross and consequently the paper's owner and editor, David Astor, offered double what the *Sunday Times* had bid.

So began the Great Waugh Boom. For eight weeks, an unprecedented stretch, juicy extracts chosen by Michael Davie appeared in the *Observer*'s colour magazine, boosting the paper's circulation and reawakening an interest in Evelyn's life and work that continues to this day. Davie went on to edit a bestselling book of Evelyn's diaries, and in 1980 a selection of his letters was published (others were to follow).

It is a measure of how Evelyn's stock had risen that the *Observer* paid double what it had for the diaries to serialize the letters. The following year Granada Television's eleven-part dramatization of *Brideshead Revisited* was shown, since when there have been several more adaptations of his work for film and television. Meanwhile although Evelyn himself is regarded as, at best, a bizarre museum piece, his novels continue to sell briskly. Why should this be? Evelyn provides the answer in an article he wrote on literary style: 'Style is what makes a work memorable and unmistakable. We remember the false judgments of Voltaire and Gibbon and Lytton Strachey long after they have been corrected because of their sharp polished form and because of the sensual pleasure of dwelling on them.'

To Voltaire, Gibbon and Lytton Strachey we can add the name of Evelyn Waugh.

Notes

1. For his part Cruttwell described Evelyn as 'a silly little suburban snob with an inferiority complex and no palate'.

2. Probably because they described his homosexual activities.

3. Mrs Lewis was unimpressed by Evelyn's depiction of her as Lottie Crump in *Vile Bodies*, saying she'd 'cut 'is winkle orf' if their paths crossed again.

4. Auberon Waugh rejected his father's avowal. He thought that without his faith Evelyn might have been 'less strictly charitable, but a much nicer man to know'.

5. Strangely, almost the only literary allusion to be found in Evelyn's fiction is a reference to Proust's character Charlus, with whom Mr Samgrass spends 'a cozy afternoon before the fire' at Brideshead.

6. She was the widow of Aubrey Herbert (1880–1923), a colourful diplomat and intelligence officer who was twice offered the throne of Albania and who is reputedly the model for Sandy Arbuthnot in John Buchan's *Greenmantle*.

7. They were not divorced until 1958.

8. Winston Churchill, contracted to write his history of the Second World War, was equally cheesed off. 'I'm not going to work when they take nineteen and six out of every pound,' he grumbled to his doctor, Lord Moran, in August 1945.

9. Evelyn was by no means the only writer to profit from such a wheeze. Other beneficiaries included Dennis Wheatley and Ian Fleming.

10. Legend has it that Bron, *in extremis*, said 'Kiss me, Chudleigh' to his Corporal of Horse.

11. Sykes might also have mentioned that the Old Hundredth was what Evelyn called the nightclub Ryder, Sebastian and Boy Mulcaster visit in *Brideshead*.

Acknowledgements

First, I must thank three American academics: Dr John Wilson, editor of the Evelyn Waugh Society newsletter, for his prompt and informative replies to my queries; Richard Oram, of the Harry Ransom Centre at the University of Texas, for information about Evelyn Waugh as book collector; and Nicholas Scheetz, curator of manuscripts at Georgetown University Library, for correspondence between Hugh Trevor-Roper and Christopher Sykes. I am also very grateful to Alexander Waugh for information about the sale of his grandfather's library and the copy of a press cutting from the Evening Standard. For the story of how Evelyn Waugh's Diaries came to be serialized in the Observer I must thank Donald Trelford, Anne Chisholm and Michael Sissons.

A large collection of letters to Evelyn Waugh can be found at the British Library. For easy access to books by, and about, Waugh, there is nowhere to beat the London Library.

My editor at Hesperus, Robin Harries, has been most supportive, particularly with regard to editing online. And, as always, I must acknowledge the forbearance of my wife, Susanna.

Works by Evelyn Waugh

In his lifetime Waugh had four British publishers: Chapman and Hall, Duckworth, Longman and Penguin, the last of whom have published several editions of his work. *Sword of Honour*, with an introduction by Frank Kermode, is also available under the Everyman's Library imprint. A complete edition of Waugh's work is to be published by Oxford University Press in 2015.

In America, Waugh's early works were published by Cape, Smith and Farrar & Rinehart. From 1938 onwards he was published by Little, Brown. Dates given below are for the British editions.

Fiction

Decline and Fall (1928)
Vile Bodies (1930)
Black Mischief (1932)
A Handful of Dust (1934)
Mr Loveday's Little Outing and Other Sad Stories (1936)
Scoop (1938)
Put Out More Flags (1942)
Work Suspended (1942)
Brideshead Revisited (1945)
Scott-King's Modern Europe (1947)
The Loved One (1948)
Helena (1950)
Men At Arms (1952)
Love Among the Ruins (1953)
Officers and Gentlemen (1955)
The Ordeal of Gilbert Pinfold (1957)
Unconditional Surrender (1961)
Basil Seal Rides Again (1963)
Sword of Honour – a final version of the war trilogy (1965)

Non-Fiction

Rossetti, His Life and Works (1928)
Labels (1930)
Remote People (1931)
Ninety-Two Days (1934)
Edmund Campion: Jesuit and Martyr (1935)
Waugh in Abyssinia (1936)
Robbery Under Law (1939)
When the Going Was Good (1946)
The Life of the Right Reverend Ronald Knox (1959)
A Tourist in Africa (1960)
A Little Learning (1964)

Posthumously published works

Michael Davie (ed.), *The Diaries of Evelyn Waugh* (London, 1976)
Mark Amory (ed.), *The Letters of Evelyn Waugh* (London, 1980)
Donat Gallagher (ed.), *The Essays, Articles and Reviews of Evelyn Waugh* (London, 1983)

Select bibliography

Evelyn Waugh has been the subject of several biographies, some aimed at the general reader, others at the specialist. To date, the only one that bridges the gap is Martin Stannard's comprehensive double-decker. Unlike Christopher Sykes, Stannard took the trouble to talk to Waugh's first wife, Evelyn Nightingale. He is also very good on the sordid topic of money. That said, there are those who think that despite his diligence, Stannard misses the point of Waugh. They prefer Selina Hastings' Life, on the slightly snooty grounds that, as Anthony Powell observed, 'She possesses the immense advantage of knowing who and what one is talking about.' Powell himself has some very pertinent things to say about Waugh, both as a writer and as a man, but latterly his loathing for Bron Waugh spoils the effect. Arguably the most engaging book about Waugh is Frances Donaldson's portrait of him as a country neighbour. His warts are visible, but so is his appeal.

Harold Acton, *Memoirs of an Aesthete* (London, 1948)
Harold Acton, *Nancy Mitford* (London, 1976)
Kingsley Amis, *The Amis Collection* (London, 1990)
Mark Amory (ed.) *The Letters of Ann Fleming* (London, 1985)
Mark Amory (ed.) *The Letters of Evelyn Waugh* (London, 1980)
Noel Annan, *Our Age* (London, 1990)
Noel Annan, *Roxburgh of Stowe* (London, 1965)
Malcolm Bradbury, *Evelyn Waugh* (London, 1964)
Michael Barber, *Anthony Powell: A Life* (London, 2005)
Antony Beevor, *Crete: The Battle and the Resistance* (London, 1990)
Maurice Bowra, *Memories 1898–1939* (London, 1969)
John Bright-Holmes (ed.) *Like It Was: The Diaries of Malcolm Muggeridge* (London 1981)
Jimmy Burns, *Papa Spy* (London, 2009)
Paula Byrne, *Mad World: Evelyn Waugh and the secrets of Brideshead* (London, 2009)

Dudley Carew, *A Fragment of Friendship* (London, 1974)

Humphrey Carpenter, *The Brideshead Generation* (London, 1989)

Artemis Cooper, *Cairo in the War 1939–1945* (London, 1989)

Artemis Cooper (ed.), *Mr Wu and Mrs Stitch: The Letters of Evelyn Waugh and Diana Cooper* (London, 1991)

Valentine Cunningham, *British Writers of the Thirties* (London, 1988)

Michael Davie, *The Diaries of Evelyn Waugh* (London,1976)

Frances Donaldson, *Evelyn Waugh: Portrait of a Country Neighbour* (London, 1967)

Tom Driberg, *Ruling Passions* (London, 1977)

Paul Fussell, *Abroad* (London, 1980)

Donat Gallagher, *The Essays, Articles and Reviews of Evelyn Waugh* (London, 1984)

Martin Green, *Children of the Sun* (London, 1977)

Graham Greene, *Ways of Escape* (London, 1980)

Selina Hastings, *Evelyn Waugh* (London, 1994)

Shirley Hazzard, *Greene on Capri* (London, 2000)

Jeffrey Heath, *The Picturesque Prison* (London, 1982)

Christopher Hollis, *Oxford in the Twenties* (London, 1974)

Richard Johnstone, *The Will to Believe* (London, 1982)

Jeremy Lewis, *Cyril Connolly* (London, 1997)

Leslie Mitchell, *Maurice Bowra* (London, 2009)

Charlotte Mosley (ed.), *The Letters of Nancy Mitford and Evelyn Waugh* (London, 1996)

Malcolm Muggeridge, *Chronicles of Wasted Time, Vol. 2* (London 1973)

Norman Page, *An Evelyn Waugh Chronology* (London 1997)

David Pryce-Jones (ed.), *Evelyn Waugh and His World* (London, 1973)

Anthony Powell, *To Keep the Ball Rolling, Vols. 1–4* (London 1976–82)

Anthony Powell, *Journals 1982–1992, 3 Vols.* (London 1995–1997)

Anthony Powell, *Miscellaneous Verdicts* (London, 1990)

Violet Powell, *The Departure Platform* (London 1996)

Peter Quennell, *The Marble Foot* (London 1976)

Peter Quennell, *The Wanton Chase* (London, 1980)

Charles Ritchie, *The Siren Years* (London, 1974)

Stephen Robertson, *The Remarkable Lives of Bill Deedes*
(London, 2007)

A.L. Rowse, *Memories and Glimpses* (London, 1986)

Wilfrid Sheed, *The Good Word* (London, 1979)

Martin Stannard (ed.), *Evelyn Waugh: The Critical Heritage*
(London, 1984)

Martin Stannard, *Evelyn Waugh: The Early Years 1903–1939*
(London 1986)

Martin Stannard, *Evelyn Waugh: No Abiding City 1939–1966*
(London 1992)

Frederick J. Stopp, *Evelyn Waugh, Portrait of an Artist*
(London, 1958)

Christopher Sykes, *Evelyn Waugh: A Biography* (London, 1975)

D.J. Taylor, *Bright Young People* (London, 2007)

Alec Waugh, *The Early Years of Alec Waugh* (London 1962)

Alec Waugh, *My Brother Evelyn and Other Profiles*
(London, 1967)

Alec Waugh, *The Best Wine Last* (London, 1978)

Alexander Waugh, *Fathers and Sons* (London, 2004)

Auberon Waugh, *Will This Do?* (London, 1991)

Francis Wheen, *Tom Driberg: His Life and Indiscretions*
(London 1990)

Edmund Wilson, *Classics and Commercials* (London, 1951)

Essays, Articles and Reviews

'Three evocations of Evelyn Waugh by Anthony Powell,
Harold Acton and John Sutro' (*Adam International Review*,
1966, Nos. 301-302-303.)

'Evelyn Waugh – A Brief Life', narrated by Christopher
Sykes, with contributions from Waugh's friends and
contemporaries (*The Listener*, 24.8.1967)

'A Critique of Waugh, with contributions from Christopher Sykes, Cyril Connolly, Raymond Mortimer and Goronwy Rees' (*The Listener*, 31.8.1967)

John Banville, 'The Family Pinfold' (*New York Review of Books*, 28.6.2007)

John Bayley, 'Blacking' (*London Review of Books*, 4.12.1986)

John Bayley, 'The Black Wizard's Spell' (*Times Literary Supplement*, 24.4.1992)

John Carey, 'Hell's Angel' (*Sunday Times*, 19.4.1992)

Claud Cockburn, 'Evelyn Waugh's Lost Rabbit' (*Atlantic Monthly*, December 1973)

Graham Greene, 'Both Dross and Gold' (*Books and Bookmen*, August 1976)

Christopher Hitchens, 'The Permanent Adolescent' (*Atlantic Monthly*, May 2003)

Julian Jebb, 'Writers at Work: Evelyn Waugh', (*Paris Review*, Issue 30)

Conor Cruise O'Brien, 'Nobs and Snobs' (*New York Review of Books*, 4. 2. 1988)

Simon Raven, 'Crusader of our Time' (*London Magazine*, November 1961)

Wilfrid Sheed, 'Portrait of the Artist as a Self-Made Man' (*New York Review of Books*, 16.12.93)

Geoffrey Wheatcroft, 'A Prophet Without Honour' (*Times Literary Supplement*, 24.10.2003)

Biographical note

Michael Barber has spent forty years writing and broadcasting about books and writers. He is the author of *The Captain: the Life and Times of Simon Raven* (London, 1996) and *Anthony Powell: A Life* (London, 2004). Married, with a son, a stepson and a step-daughter, he lives in Wimbledon.

HESPERUS PRESS

Hesperus Press is committed to bringing near what is far – far both in space and time. Works written by the greatest authors, and unjustly neglected or simply little known in the English-speaking world, are made accessible through new translations and a completely fresh editorial approach. Through these classic works, the reader is introduced to the greatest writers from all times and all cultures.

For more information on Hesperus Press, please visit our website: **www.hesperuspress.com**

SELECTED TITLES FROM HESPERUS PRESS

Author	Title	Foreword writer
Pietro Aretino	*The School of Whoredom*	Paul Bailey
Pietro Aretino	*The Secret Life of Nuns*	
Jane Austen	*Lesley Castle*	Zoë Heller
Jane Austen	*Love and Friendship*	Fay Weldon
Honoré de Balzac	*Colonel Chabert*	A.N. Wilson
Charles Baudelaire	*On Wine and Hashish*	Margaret Drabble
Giovanni Boccaccio	*Life of Dante*	A.N. Wilson
Charlotte Brontë	*The Spell*	
Emily Brontë	*Poems of Solitude*	Helen Dunmore
Mikhail Bulgakov	*Fatal Eggs*	Doris Lessing
Mikhail Bulgakov	*The Heart of a Dog*	A.S. Byatt
Giacomo Casanova	*The Duel*	Tim Parks
Miguel de Cervantes	*The Dialogue of the Dogs*	Ben Okri
Geoffrey Chaucer	*The Parliament of Birds*	
Anton Chekhov	*The Story of a Nobody*	Louis de Bernières
Anton Chekhov	*Three Years*	William Fiennes
Wilkie Collins	*The Frozen Deep*	
Joseph Conrad	*Heart of Darkness*	A.N. Wilson
Joseph Conrad	*The Return*	Colm Tóibín
Gabriele D'Annunzio	*The Book of the Virgins*	Tim Parks
Dante Alighieri	*The Divine Comedy: Inferno*	
Dante Alighieri	*New Life*	Louis de Bernières
Daniel Defoe	*The King of Pirates*	Peter Ackroyd
Marquis de Sade	*Incest*	Janet Street-Porter
Charles Dickens	*The Haunted House*	Peter Ackroyd
Charles Dickens	*A House to Let*	
Fyodor Dostoevsky	*The Double*	Jeremy Dyson
Fyodor Dostoevsky	*Poor People*	Charlotte Hobson
Alexandre Dumas	*One Thousand and One Ghosts*	

George Eliot	*Amos Barton*	Matthew Sweet
Henry Fielding	*Jonathan Wild the Great*	Peter Ackroyd
F. Scott Fitzgerald	*The Popular Girl*	Helen Dunmore
Gustave Flaubert	*Memoirs of a Madman*	Germaine Greer
Ugo Foscolo	*Last Letters of Jacopo Ortis*	Valerio Massimo Manfredi
Elizabeth Gaskell	*Lois the Witch*	Jenny Uglow
Théophile Gautier	*The Jinx*	Gilbert Adair
André Gide	*Theseus*	
Johann Wolfgang von Goethe	*The Man of Fifty*	A.S. Byatt
Nikolai Gogol	*The Squabble*	Patrick McCabe
E.T.A. Hoffmann	*Mademoiselle de Scudéri*	Gilbert Adair
Victor Hugo	*The Last Day of a Condemned Man*	Libby Purves
Joris-Karl Huysmans	*With the Flow*	Simon Callow
Henry James	*In the Cage*	Libby Purves
Franz Kafka	*Metamorphosis*	Martin Jarvis
Franz Kafka	*The Trial*	Zadie Smith
John Keats	*Fugitive Poems*	Andrew Motion
Heinrich von Kleist	*The Marquise of O–*	Andrew Miller
Mikhail Lermontov	*A Hero of Our Time*	Doris Lessing
Nikolai Leskov	*Lady Macbeth of Mtsensk*	Gilbert Adair
Carlo Levi	*Words are Stones*	Anita Desai
Xavier de Maistre	*A Journey Around my Room*	Alain de Botton
André Malraux	*The Way of the Kings*	Rachel Seiffert
Katherine Mansfield	*Prelude*	William Boyd
Edgar Lee Masters	*Spoon River Anthology*	Shena Mackay
Guy de Maupassant	*Butterball*	Germaine Greer
Prosper Mérimée	*Carmen*	Philip Pullman
Sir Thomas More	*The History of King Richard III*	Sister Wendy Beckett
Sándor Petőfi	*John the Valiant*	George Szirtes

Francis Petrarch	*My Secret Book*	Germaine Greer
Luigi Pirandello	*Loveless Love*	
Edgar Allan Poe	*Eureka*	Sir Patrick Moore
Alexander Pope	*The Rape of the Lock and A Key to the Lock*	Peter Ackroyd
Antoine-François Prévost	*Manon Lescaut*	Germaine Greer
Marcel Proust	*Pleasures and Days*	A.N. Wilson
Alexander Pushkin	*Dubrovsky*	Patrick Neate
Alexander Pushkin	*Ruslan and Lyudmila*	Colm Tóibín
François Rabelais	*Pantagruel*	Paul Bailey
François Rabelais	*Gargantua*	Paul Bailey
Christina Rossetti	*Commonplace*	Andrew Motion
George Sand	*The Devil's Pool*	Victoria Glendinning
Jean-Paul Sartre	*The Wall*	Justin Cartwright
Friedrich von Schiller	*The Ghost-seer*	Martin Jarvis
Mary Shelley	*Transformation*	
Percy Bysshe Shelley	*Zastrozzi*	Germaine Greer
Stendhal	*Memoirs of an Egotist*	Doris Lessing
Stendhal	*On Love*	A.C. Grayling
Robert Louis Stevenson	*Dr Jekyll and Mr Hyde*	Helen Dunmore
Theodor Storm	*The Lake of the Bees*	Alan Sillitoe
Leo Tolstoy	*The Death of Ivan Ilych*	
Leo Tolstoy	*Hadji Murat*	Colm Tóibín
Ivan Turgenev	*Faust*	Simon Callow
Mark Twain	*The Diary of Adam and Eve*	John Updike
Mark Twain	*Tom Sawyer, Detective*	
Oscar Wilde	*The Portrait of Mr W.H.*	Peter Ackroyd
Virginia Woolf	*Carlyle's House and Other Sketches*	Doris Lessing
Virginia Woolf	*Monday or Tuesday*	Scarlett Thomas
Emile Zola	*For a Night of Love*	A.N. Wilson